Pioneer Mixology:
Switchel, Sack Posset, and Shrub

A Survey of Prairie Beverages

Robynne Elizabeth Miller

DEDICATION

To Brooke Mardell and Jackie Knapp.

For the name. For the encouragement. For the laughter.

But, mostly, for the name. ☺

And, of course, to Ian. Because.

CONTENTS

ACKNOWLEDGMENTS

This was a funny little project, with lots of rabbit trails of research
and investigation. Many people helped me along the way, and
I am extremely grateful to all of the librarians, research assistants
and history buffs who put up with my endless questions. Thank you all.

A very special thank you goes to Ian Feavearyear. Without his help with research, formatting, and editing, this book would be a mess!

But, mostly, I appreciate the time and encouragement my
precious husband and family offered every step of the way!

INTRODUCTION

Pioneer literature isn't exactly overrun with references to the beverages of the time. Throughout the *Little House* series, by Laura Ingalls Wilder, for example, the few references mentioned in the entire nine books, spanning about 20 years of pioneer life, are to such things as water, milk, coffee, tea, lemonade, ginger water (switchel), apple cider and a brief nod to eggnog.

But was that an exhaustive list? Not by a long shot!

While those who write about pioneers seem to overlook the importance of consuming liquid, publications of the period did not. To be fair, moving away from settled cities and towns probably did curtail the number and variety of drinks available, mostly due to financial constraints. . .pioneers usually weren't terribly flush with cash. And ingredients, especially rare ones like lemons, were costly. References in periodicals, cookbooks and other historical data suggest that there were quite a few interesting drinks floating around in the mid 19th century.

And that's exactly what I want to explore!

So what kinds of pioneer beverages are we talking about?

Three major categories:

Hot: Coffee and its MANY substitutes, Beef Tea, Mulled Cider (non-alcoholic), Chocolate/Cocoa, Steamed Milk, Cambric Tea, and Herb and traditional Teas

Cold: Lemonade, Pioneer Lemonade, Switchel, Cider, Milk, Buttermilk, Whey, Ginger Beer/Ginger Ale, Root Beer

Alcoholic: Cordials, Punch, Eggnog, Egg Caudle, Mulled Cider (alcoholic), Ale, Hard Cider, Wine, Syllabub, Sack Posset and Shrub

Though some of these drinks were certainly tasty and considered a special treat, liquid, in general, was definitely not considered merely a luxury to the pioneers. Listen to this famous trail guide:

> "Very few cooking utensils, should be taken, as they very much increase the load, to avoid which, is always a consideration of paramount importance. A baking-kettle, frying-pan, tea-kettle, tea-pot, and coffee-pot, are all the furniture of this kind, that is essential" (Hastings, 1845, p. 144)

Since three of five cooking implements suggested were for the making of beverages, we can pretty easily surmise that beverages were not an afterthought to the pioneers. They were pretty dang important!

But how did they make their drinks? What were period recipes? How did they procure the necessary ingredients? What were the methods they used? What's the history and value and usage behind what they consumed???

These are questions I want to *know*! I hope you do, too. It's actually pretty darn interesting stuff!

PART 1:

Hot

HOT DRINKS

Something hot on a cold day always sounds good. For settlers, however, a steaming beverage was a matter of safety as well. Before a well could be dug, which offered the cleanest possible drinking water, sources could be anything from a river, a stream, a lake, a pond or even rain runoff from the roof (which was often made of sod or wood shingles!!).

Though folks of that day often had sturdier stomachs due to constant exposure to various microorganisms and healthy gut bacteria we largely avoid in the modern day, water from natural sources wasn't always the best option for straight drinking even to them. Sometimes, even if it was technically "safe" to drink, it just tasted plain mucky and foul!

Hot drinks provided a masking flavor, some welcome variance from plain water, and served to make water safer and more palatable. Boiling liquid kills a number of nasty organisms that can wreak havoc on a digestive system.

No wonder there are a lot of options in the 'hot drinks' category!

TEA

Tea has been around for centuries, originating in China sometime around 1500 BC. Great Britain became thoroughly enamored with it in the 17th century and, by 1750, it was considered the national drink. Being initially populated by a large proportion of British ex-pats, Americans followed suit with their love for tea.

Until the crown levied a huge tax on the transportation and sale of tea, that is. (Which didn't go over so well with the colonists, as I'm sure you remember from grammar school history!)

In protest, and despite their passionate love for tea, Americans largely stopped drinking it. Eventually, the whole ugly Boston Tea Party and American Revolution thing happened, and tea became more than a form of protest. . .it was decidedly un-patriotic there for awhile.

Several tea substitutes were explored during this period, including steeping goldenrod, strawberry and blackberry leaves, as well as rhubarb and dried raspberry leaves (called 'Balsamic Hyperion'). Sassafras Tea was also quite popular. Not fantastic substitutes for the real thing, mind you, but a strong testimony to the patriotism and resolve of the young Americans who would do just about anything to avoid drinking the patron drink of the Brits.

Here's one recipe for a cold tea substitute, said to be good for bringing down fevers or cooling down anyone who has become overheated:

Balm and Burrage Tea

Ingredients:

- Small Handful of Balm
- Small Handful of Burrage
- 1 Quart Water, boiling
- Pot
- Strainer

Method:

- Wash and pat dry all leaves.
- When clean, crush slightly and place in teapot.
- Add boiling water and steep for 8-10 minutes.
- Strain leaves and allow tea to cool.
- Serve at either room temperature or over ice.
- Refreshing!

Thankfully, after the war ended and America declared its independence from Britain, tea began to very slowly seep its way back into favor. It never quite regained the popularity it had before the war, though, largely because coffee had stepped resoundingly into its place. By the mid-1800's, however, the pioneers could hardly remember the whole tea kerfuffle and it was no longer politically, morally, or socially unacceptable to drink it.

I'm married to a Brit, who very carefully taught me the secret of making a "proper pot of tea." Our bi-cultural marriage might have been considered high treason at one point, but I feel on fairly safe ground now. So I don't mind sharing that little secret with you:

Perfect Pot of Tea

Ingredients:

- One generous teaspoon of loose leaf tea per cup, plus one for the pot if you're making at least 6 cups of tea
- Fresh water, preferably artesian spring rather than tap, freshly boiled, 6 ounces per cup
- Pot that holds at least 6-8 cups
- Tea strainer, clean muslin, or very fine sieve
- Tea cozy or clean towel
- Milk and sugar, optional to taste

Method:

- Warm your pot by adding very hot water to it and letting it stand for five minutes while water boils in a separate kettle.
- Drain water from teapot and add tea leaves.
- Pour in water that had been brought to a vigorous boil and then rested for one minute.
- Do not stir the tea leaves.
- Place the lid on the pot and wrap in a cozy or towel.
- Steep for no more than 3 minutes.
- Strain tea into cups via tea strainer, muslin or fine mesh sieve.
- Add sugar and milk if desired

Cambric Tea/Nursery Tea

When I first read the *Little House on the Prairie* series, way back when I was a little girl, I was intrigued by the author's description of much younger children excitedly wanting to drink tea, and puzzled by how much grownups seemed to think it was inappropriate. The cost of tea may have been more of a factor than whether or not it was perceived to have been inappropriate for children. . .especially since 'special occasions' did warrant a child's version of the adult beverage: Cambric Tea. Since the children receiving said treat always seemed happy to do so, and felt very grown up besides, I couldn't wait to try it myself. I was only eight at the time, after all.

Although the Internet wasn't around in its current form back then, I did find resources that expounded on the recipe slightly more than the description in the *Little House* books, but I never knew much about the history of the drink. Thankfully, we now have a world of information at our fingertips, and the website, wiseGeek, puts the history beautifully into perspective:

> The American authoress Laura Ingalls Wilder makes several references in her *Little House* series to a favorite hot beverage known as *cambric tea* or *nursery tea*. Cambric tea is a "children's tea" made primarily from sugar, hot water, heated milk or cream and perhaps a dash or two of strongly brewed tea. This weak tea generally serves as the beverage of choice in a child's tea party, or becomes the introduction to stronger beverages such as regular tea or coffee.

> Cambric tea derives its name from a resemblance to cambric cloth, a very thin white fabric often used to make lightweight garments. It is believed that the French were the first to develop cambric tea, most likely as an alternative to the strong teas generally reserved for healthy adults. Cambric tea was deemed suitable for young children, invalids and the elderly, since it did not contain any caffeine or other troubling ingredients.

The popularity of cambric tea during the 18th and 19th centuries was largely due to the availability of its basic ingredients. While adults often packed supplies of coffee and tea during their long treks towards the West, these beverages were considered too harsh for children. Fresh milk or cream, however, could be obtained from dairy cows on many farms, and loaf sugar could be purchased in mercantile stores along the way. Therefore, cambric tea became a popular beverage among pioneer children such as Laura Ingalls Wilder. (wiseGEEK, *What is Cambric Tea*)

Cambric Tea

Ingredients:

- ¼ cup milk or cream, cold
- ¾ cup hot water
- 1-2 tablespoons prepared tea (liquid tea, already brewed)
- 2-3 teaspoons light brown sugar

Method:

- Mix hot water, tea and sugar in mug or teacup
- When sugar is dissolved, add cold milk or cream and stir
- Taste and adjust as necessary
- Make sure that the beverage is warm, but not hot, before giving to child.
- Enjoy!

BEEF TEA

I've seen references to Beef Tea across a number of sources. It's mentioned in literature far pre-dating the Great Westward Movement, and afterwards as well. It's been mentioned in period dramas, newspaper and magazine articles, and makes an appearance in most recipe collections published anywhere near the period, including:

- The Cooking Manual of Practical Directions for Economical Every-Day Cookery (1877)

- A Plain Cookery Book for the Working Classes (1852)

- Directions for Cookery, in its Various Branches (1840 or 1849?)

- Fifty Soups (1884)

- The Book of Household Management (1861)

- The White House Cookbook (1887)

So, what is it, then? Essentially, it's a concentrated beef broth made from nothing more than very lean beef, water, and sometimes a little salt. It's the home made precursor to Bovril and other granulated beef bouillons, which we now use mainly in recipes to enrich the beefy flavor rather than to improve health.

While teas now have connotations of helping us to unwind and relax in the midst of a busy day, Beef Tea was strictly medicinal back in the day. It was thought to be hugely beneficial to those who were ill or weak from a plethora of maladies. Capturing the essence of beef, and delivering it to a patient via a gentle, easily tolerated broth, was _the_ go-to food in nursing anyone back to health, for virtually any medical condition. (Apparently, even Florence Nightingale used it to nurse wounded soldiers back to health!)

Variations did allow for other meats to be used, such as lamb or chicken, but beef was definitely preferred. Some later recipes also included vegetables in the steeping process, but the purest form of the recipe is simply beef and water. Go beyond that and you have soup, really.

Interestingly, a period article from the New York Times (which you can easily find online if you've got a mind to Google it!) discusses the enormous waste generated in the making of Beef Tea. One pound of meat produced only a measly pint of tea if you use the boiling method and only 4 or 5 ounces of tea if you use the steeping method. After extracting so little, the beef was then discarded as it was believed to no longer hold any value. . .the essence, it was thought, had been leached out into the liquid! That is some expensive, expensive tea!! Here is what the part of the article says:

> The waste of beef in making beef tea is enormous. 62,000 lbs.
> a year are used in one London hospital alone; and if any head
> of a household, where there has been long illness, will just
> sum up the addition to the Butcher's bill in the shape of beef
> tea meat, he will be able to form some notion of the quantity
> used, and (many of the doctors are beginning to tell us) more
> than half wasted, throughout the country. At the present price
> of meat this is a very serious matter. It is LIEBIG's theory that
> in beef tea, properly made, you get all the nutrive part of the
> beef, and leave nothing but a worthless mass of bouilli behind.
> (NY Times, July 16, 1865)

That's a lot of wasted beef! However, staunch advocates stood firm: the cost and waste were far outweighed by the health benefit to the patient. In a time of limited medicinal options, I suppose proponents had a point. It was easily tolerated, fairly nutritious, and would often 'go down' when other things wouldn't.

Here are two recipes, one using a 'steeping' method and the other 'boiling' the beef:

Beef Tea, Steeped

Ingredients:

- 1 pound very lean beef
- Sprinkle of salt
- Wide mouthed glass or stone jar, with tight cork
- Pan large enough to accommodate jar and water
- Water
- Bowl
- Muslin or Fine Strainer

Method:

- Slice beef into very thin slices.
- Sprinkle a tiny bit of salt over them.
- Place meat in jar and cork or seal tightly.
- Set in pan and add water so that it comes up to the line of beef inside the jar.
- Bring to the boil and maintain a boil for at least an hour, preferably two.
- Make sure boiling water always stays level with the beef.
- Remove jar (carefully, as it's very hot!!) from the pot.
- Strain the beef, capturing the liquid (tea) in a bowl and pressing out any extra from the meat.
- Discard beef and serve the tea.

Beef Tea, Boiled

Ingredients:

- 1 pound lean beef
- Sprinkle of salt
- Saucepan
- 1 Quart of Water
- Bowl
- Muslin or Fine Strainer

Method:

- Finely chop the beef.
- Add beef and water to the saucepan.
- Bring it up to a fast boil, stirring occasionally.
- Once at a boil, boil rapidly for ten to fifteen minutes.
- Strain and discard beef, pressing out all liquid possible.
- Salt to taste.
- Serve, either alone or with dry toast.

A little later, variations started appearing, including ones that added spices and vegetables. Much to the chagrin of purists, who believed that it was the simple essence of the beef which provided nutrition in a form that was easily tolerated by the sick, recipes like the following gained ground:

Beef Tea from Fresh Meat (Baron Liebig's Recipe) Take one pound of lean beef, entirely free from fat and sinew; mince it finely and mix it well with one pint of cold water. Put it on the hob, and let it remain heating very gradually for two hours. At the end of that time, add half a teas-spoonful of salt and boil gently for ten minutes. Remove the scum as it rises. This is beef tea pure and simple. When a change of flavour is required it is a good plan to take one pound of meat composed of equal parts of veal, mutton, and beef, and proceed as above. Or, instead of using water, boil a carrot, a turnip, an onion, and a clove, in a pint of water, and when the flavour is extracted strain the liquid trough a fine sieve; let it get quite cold, and pour it upon the minced meat, soaking and boiling it for the same time. Probable cost, 1s per pint. Sufficient for one pint of beef tea. (Food Timeline, *Beef Tea*)

For more information, the website 'Vintage Recipes' has an absolute treasure trove of recipes from numerous period cookbooks and resources. Check out their extensive section on Beef Tea. (Vintage Recipes, *Beef Tea*)

COFFEE

As popular as coffee is at the present time, it was strangely crucial to people in the 19th century as both a warming beverage and as a potential cure-all. The Food Timeline website offers a great quote from the "Family Receipt Book:"

> Virtues of Coffee: Coffee accelerates digestion corrects crudités, removes colic and flatulencies. It mitigates headaches, cherishes the animal spirits, takes away listlessness and languor, and is serviceable in all obstructions arising from languid circulation. It is a wonderful restorative to emaciated constitutions, and highly refreshing to the studious and sedentary. (Food Timeline, *Virtues of Coffee*)

Those are some potent claims! Whether coffee had actually been substantiated to serve those noble purposes, or whether it was just rhetoric to fuel merchant's marketing campaigns, I don't know. What is certain, however, is that coffee was America's hot adult beverage of choice. The Great Tea Kerfuffle of the 18th century had more than seen to that. Drinking coffee was patriotic (a royal thumb to the nose of the Crown and her Tea tax!), supposedly healthy, and downright yummy. A win-win-win!

In one of my very, very favorite books, "A Hand-Book for Overland Expeditions," which was THE definitive handbook for settlers wanting to head west to California in the mid 1800's, author Randolph B. Marcy lists what provisions are necessary for the 110 day trip:

> The allowance of provisions for each grown person, to make the journey from the Missouri River to California, should suffice for 110 days. The following is deemed requisite, viz.: 150 lbs of flour or its equivalent in hard bread; 25 lbs. of bacon or pork, and enough fresh beef to be driven on the hoof to make

up the meat component of the ration; 15 lbs. of coffee, and 25 lbs. of sugar; also a quantity or saleratus or yeast powders for making bread, and salt and pepper. (Marcy, 1993)

Did you catch that? 15 POUNDS of coffee!! *Per PERSON*!?! And this is in the midst of a huge diatribe about how nothing super-fluous should be brought on the journey, at great peril of life and limb! How, then, did 15 pounds of coffee per person rate as a *necessity*? Was it simply because water on the trail could be hazardous to one's health? Or perhaps the pioneers were caffeine addicts? Did they regard coffee as medicinal? Or was there a realization that a steaming cup of joe in the midst of a very stressful, very long journey had huge psychological, physical, and emotional benefits?

Probably it was a combination of all of those reasons, though we may never know for sure. It's clear, however, from just about every resource on the topic that coffee was not considered a luxury. It was a vital staple!

Making coffee then was not terrifically different from now. Settlers bought coffee beans green from their local mercantile. Coffee from the regions of Havana, Java and Rio were available at the time. When coffee was wanted, they were roasted just before brewing to produce the richest flavor possible. Roasting was a far more reliable process when done in an oven (stirring frequently), but could also be done in a cast iron skillet over an open campfire (though this produced slightly uneven results). Care had to be taken in both methods to achieve a rich, deep brown color and avoid burning any of the beans (which could ruin the whole brew), but, essentially, it was a fairly simple procedure.

Here's why pre-roasted beans were a thing of the future:

Not until after the Civil War did manufacturers devise a good way of preserving the flavor of pre-roasted or ground coffee, sometimes referred to as essence of coffee. But from March

30, 1850, St. Louis Missouri Republican this ad suggests that they certainly tried. 'California Outfits. Ground Coffee--Put up in water-proof and air-tight packages and guaranteed to re-tain its strength and flavor for years.' The credit for a good roasted coffee goes to Arbuckle Brothers, whose offices were in Pittsburgh, Pennsylvania. The company patented a method of sealing in the roasted flavor by coating the beans with a mixture of egg white and sugar. Roasted coffee beans in paper bags were then shipped throughout the West, and Arbuckle coffee was the most popular brand. (Food Timeline, *Pioneer Coffee*)

An interesting thing to note is that Arbuckle's Coffee is still in existence! From their website:

Up until the close of the Civil War, coffee was sold green. It had to be roasted on a wood stove or in a skillet over a camp-fire before it could be ground and brewed. One burned bean ruined all; there was no consistency. In 1865, John Arbuckle and his brother Charles, partners in a Pittsburgh grocery busi-ness, changed all this by patenting a process for roasting and coating coffee beans with an egg and sugar glaze to seal in the flavor and aroma.

Traditional Coffee Packaging

Marketed under the name ARBUCKLES' ARIOSA COFFEE®, in patented, airtight, one pound packages. The new coffee was an instant success. Chuck wagon cooks in the west were faced with the task of keeping cowboys supplied with plenty of hot coffee out on the range. ARBUCKLES' ARIOSA (air-ee-o-sa) COFFEE® packages bore a yellow la-bel with the name ARBUCKLES' in large red letters across the front, beneath which flew a Flying Angel trademark over the words ARIOSA COFFEE® in black letters. Shipped all over the country in sturdy wooden crates, one hundred packages to a crate, ARBUCKLES' ARIOSA COFFEE® became so dominant, particularly in the west, that many cowboys were not aware there was any other kind. (Arbuckle Coffee Traders)

If you're wanting a "pre-1865" coffee experience, or just game to give roasting the pioneer way a try, there are two primary options: Open Roasting Over a Campfire and Oven Roasting (though even that's cheating a bit because a wood fired oven back then didn't give even heat, nor could the exact temperature be set!)

Roasting Green Coffee Beans

Ingredients/Equipment:

- Green Coffee beans of your choice, 1 tablespoon per desired serving
- Baking sheet or cast iron skillet
- Colander or other heat proof container
- Pot holders
- Long handled spoon
- Hard surface (to test beans for doneness)
- Heating source, such as a hot oven or open campfire/stove

Method:

Oven:

- Preheat oven to 475 degrees
- Measure desired amount of beans (1 full tablespoon per

serving of coffee)
- Spread beans in a single layer on a baking sheet
- Place in hot oven for approximately 8-10 minutes, depending on desired roast
- Stir a couple of times during roasting process with long handled spoon
- Test for doneness by attempting to crush a bean under your thumb on a hard surface. When it crushes easily, it's ready.
- Remove from oven and cool in colander
- Shake to remove chaff
- Grind

Skillet:

- Measure desired amount of beans
- Spread in a single layer in a heavy skillet
- Place over a hot fire or high heat, stirring frequently to prevent burning
- Cook 15-20 minutes, depending on desired roast
- Test for doneness at the 10 minute mark by attempting to crush a bean under your thumb on a hard surface. When it crushes easily, it's ready.
- Remove from oven and cool in colander
- Shake to remove chaff
- Grind

Campfire Coffee

Ingredients/Equipment:

- 1 Tablespoon of freshly roasted whole coffee beans per 6 ounce cup of coffee desired
- Enameled coffee pot

- 6 ounces of water per portion
- Grinder, cups
- Milk and sugar, optional

Method:

- Grind or crush coffee beans by preferred method (grinder, mortar and pestle, etc.) until you have coarse grounds
- Each tablespoon of roasted beans should yield approximately two tablespoons of ground coffee
- Add grounds to pot and add cold water (6 oz per serving)
- Bring to a boil over a high heat for approximately 3-5 minutes. Do not boil longer than that.
- Remove from heat, carefully swirl pot to settle grounds
- Pour into cups and add milk or sugar as desired

Interesting Coffee Fact: Did you know that Iced Coffee is NOT a modern invention? Here's one explanation from the InfoBarrel website:

One of iced coffee's main roots stems back to the 17th century in Vienna. After the Turkish army unsuccessfully besieged the city of Vienna, they left behind a substantial surplus of coffee beans. Perhaps having too much of a "good thing" led the Viennese into experimenting with different variations of the increasingly popular brew. Hence with the opposite of hot came, well, let's try it cold. Plus it probably helped having the Alps as abundant supply of ice/snow to mix in with their beverages. A bit of a stretch on that one I think but worth a shot.

The strongest link to the origins of iced coffee however seem to revert back to a French concoction known as mazagran. Mazagran is a cold coffee beverage made with strong coffee, lemon, ice and sometimes rum. It was all the rage in the 19th century as the drink was seen to be slightly risqué, Ou la la! (InfoBarrel)

And here is a great quote from the New York Times (from the Food Timeline website):

It is now 1 o'clock, the Court has retired--we will take one more dance...and cool off with an iced coffee and a glass of champagne (not a bad mixture) and go home. (Food Timeline, *Iced Coffee*)

Settling the Grounds

Much debate has occurred over settling the coffee grounds. Today, we have brilliant filters and presses which do the job of producing fairly clear, grit free coffees for us. But back in the day when such luxuries were not available, various methods were employed to try to keep coffee grounds and sediment out of the cup. Here's an excerpt which quotes the book 'Uncommon Grounds:'

Housewives usually brewed coffee just by boiling the grounds in water. In order to clarify the drink, or "settle" the grounds to the bottom, brewers employed various questionable additives, including eggs, fish, and eel skins...The routine American ruination of coffee must have surprised sophisticated European visitors. (Food Timeline, *Early Am. brewing*)

Wow! "*American ruination of coffee?*" That's a bit of a scathing accusation! But then again, adding eel skins? Maybe they had a point!

Here are a few (sometimes dodgy!) pioneer methods in detail:

~Swirling the pot. . .the simplest option is to gently swirl the pot (being very careful as it's extremely hot!!) to try to settle (concentrate) the grounds at the bottom. While the swirling action is still in motion, carefully pour a cup.

~Fish Skin. I have to confess that I wonder who would ever think to marry coffee and fish parts. However, it was widely used, so I am assuming it did not make the coffee taste fishy. Or that they didn't really care. Eel skins could be used in the same way. How?

Add a washed and thoroughly dried piece of fish or eel skin, about the size of a quarter, to the pot after boiling and it's supposed to both clarify the coffee as well as settle the grounds to the bottom of the pot.

~Isinglass. Now here's an interesting ingredient. While I have absolutely no idea who first thought it a great idea to try adding fish skin to coffee, I am beyond dumbfounded that anyone would consider using isinglass for the same purpose. Vikings are credited with it, but I honestly can't imagine what prompted someone, Viking or otherwise, to try it for the first time!

What is isinglass you ask? The swim bladder of a sturgeon, of course! Yes, you read that right! Originally used to settle sediment in wine and beer (again, may I ask, who decided to try this the very first time?!??!) it can be used in coffee as well. I'll leave you to decide whether you want to give this option a whirl!

If you're interested in this rather whacky option, here's a recipe citing the actual use of isinglass. It's quoted from "*Mackenzie's 5000 Recipes*" [sic.] but the edition is unclear. There's an 1829 and an 1856 version of Mackenzie's *Receipts* and the specific edition is not referenced on the Food Timeline website. Good luck finding the isinglass! Only the brave need proceed!

Coffee Milk: Boil a dessert spoonful of ground coffee in about a pint of milk, a quarter of an hour; then put into it a shaving or two of isinglass, and clear it; let it boil a few minutes, and set it on the side of the fire to fine. This is a very fine breakfast, and should be sweetened with real Lisbon sugar. Those of a spare habit, and disposed towards affections of the lungs, would do well to make this their breakfast. (Food Timeline, *Coffee Milk*)

~Rind of Salt Pork. Most chunks of salt pork, a fatty bacon-like hunk of meat, still had the rind on when it was immersed in its salty brine. Sometimes, a quarter sized piece was parboiled to remove most of the heavy salt and then added to the coffee pot when boiling. Salt pork is not smoked like regular bacon, so it certainly wouldn't add that kind of flavor, but it is incredibly salty, even after boiling, which I can't quite imagine adds much to a cup of coffee!

~Eggshells. Eggshells served two purposes when added to brewed coffee: they settled the grounds and sediment and they pulled some of the bitterness out of the coffee (eggshells are alkaline and coffee is acidic).

Here's one method:

Crush one clean eggshell for every two cups of coffee desired. Add to your pot along with coffee grounds and cold water. Bring to a boil and boil for 3-5 minutes as usual. Take off of the heat and let settle for two minutes. Carefully pour coffee into cups without disturbing sediment.

Along those same lines is a very old Norwegian recipe, which works on a somewhat similar concept to eggshells, but uses a whole egg instead:

Norwegian Egg Coffee

Ingredients/Equipment:

- Eight tablespoons of coarsely ground coffee
- 1 egg
- 6 tablespoons cold water
- 10 cups boiling water
- 1 cup cold water
- Pot
- Small bowl
- Cheesecloth, optional
- Milk, sugar, optional

Method:

- In pot, bring ten cups of water to the boil
- Combine coffee grounds and egg with 6 tablespoons cold water in small bowl
- Mix well to a thick paste
- Add coffee and egg mixture to boiling water
- Stir well, breaking up any large lumps and leave to boil for 2-3 min.
- Remove pot from heat
- Add the remaining cold water
- Let the grounds settle for two minutes
- Skim off any floating bits
- Either carefully pour into cup or filter through a cheese cloth
- Serve either as is or with cream and sugar to taste.

COFFEE SUBSTITUTES

The civilian population attacked the problem of substitutes for
coffee with a determination and energy unlike that exhibited in
the search for other expedients. No other single item had more
substitutes. The people worked at the project unceasingly,
with the result that few were the substances which did
not...find their way into a coffee pot. (Food Timeline, *Coffee
Substitutes*)

Sometimes, coffee beans just weren't available, or, if settlers
were struggling financially, affordable. But coffee was, apparently,
an absolute necessity. So what, pray tell, did the pioneers do, then?
Substitute!!

The list of possible substitutions noted in literature and period
references seems almost impossibly large. . .just about any seed or
nut or root that was edible could be roasted, ground and steeped to
make a coffee-like beverage. Even sweet potatoes were used for this
purpose! Of course, some attempts were far more successful than
others, and the results were subject to personal tastes, but the inge-
nuity of the pioneers in seeking substitutions was certainly
impressive!

When coffee was not available or was beyond the means of
the poor farmer, parched rye, chestnuts, or grape seeds were
substituted for coffee beans and brewed into hot drinks. (Food
Timeline, *Colonial American beverages: Hot, non-alcoholic*)

It was a hit and miss affair whether the attempts were even palatable, let alone pleasing, but there is evidence that many hot drinks
were actually quite delicious. General JEB Stuart, for example, is
reported to have had a marked fondness for Corn Coffee.

In some instances, as a means to stretch what real coffee beans
they did have, blends would be made out of several ingredients.

Each housewife had her own secret recipe, which she hoped was so authentic tasting that none of her guests would know wasn't pure coffee. More often, however, settlers either drank the real thing or a pure substitute.

So, what did the settlers use when real coffee was out of reach? And how did they prepare their make-shift concoctions? Read on!

Rye

Rye was probably the most common and popular runner-up to real coffee. It could be prepared in several ways, according to time and personal preference. It could be boiled and thoroughly dried, then ground just like coffee beans. Or it could be boiled, dried, roasted, and then ground. Or it could be boiled, dried, parched (roasted in a pan with a little fat until browned), and then ground. The ground rye, however you got to that point, was used in much the same way and proportion that regular ground coffee would have been.

Rye (soaked in rum)

Rye was placed in a container, soaked in rum, dried thoroughly, then roasted and ground.

These options were almost always boiled first, then dried, parched or roasted, and ground like regular coffee beans:

- Okra Seed (This was more expensive and difficult to use than rye, but it was definitely popular)
- Corn (General JEB Stuart's preference!)
- Wheat
- Peanuts
- Peas
- Chicory

- Rice
- Cotton Seed

Sweet Potato

Sweet Potatoes were "peeled and cut into 'chunks' about the size of coffee berries. The pieces were spread out in the sun to dry, then parched until brown, after which they were ground. The grounds were mixed with a little water until a paste resulted, after which hot water was added. When the grounds settled to the bottom of the coffee pot, the beverage could be poured and drunk..." (Food Timeline, *Coffee Substitutes*)

Some of the stranger possible substitutions included dandelion roots, sugar cane, sorghum molasses, beet root, regular beans, grape seeds, roasted chestnuts and, shockingly, dry brown bread crusts! The crusts were roasted and crushed to make 'grounds' which were then steeped. I can't imagine how you could get any kind of real flavor from regular beans or bread crusts, but it certainly underpins then notion that coffee, or, in desperation, its substitutes, was a crucial staple in a pioneer's diet.

Acorn Coffee

Native Americans quickly taught arriving Europeans about the wonders of the mighty acorn as a plentiful food source in America. Acorns contain tannic acid, which is not great to consume, so learning to process the nutmeats was crucial. Once that skill was mastered, however, settlers began to experiment with recipes from their homelands to find innovative uses for the new food source. One of those uses? Acorn Coffee!

Processing Acorns:

The first step in making Acorn Coffee begins with the gathering. Acorns should be harvested ripe, which means they must fall to the ground rather than plucked from the trees. Harvest in September through October. Sometimes, they will fall slightly greenish, which means they are not fully ripe. Don't worry. . .they will continue to ripen to a dark brown over the next few days.

It's very important to inspect each acorn as you gather. Look for cracks, mold, or tiny holes. Tiny holes mean that larvae are probably growing inside. Discard any that are not whole and free of blemishes. Acorns should be firm, too, so toss out any that are soft. Once you have sorted out your perfect acorns, remove the brown cap at the crown.

The next step is drying the acorns. There are several methods to doing so, from simply placing them in a single layers somewhere in your house and waiting a few weeks to using a low heat in your oven. To keep the best nut flavor and moisture, however, place your acorns in a single layer on a sheet and cover with a very thin, clean muslin or cheesecloth like material and set in the full sun, preferably inside your house near a large window. If you do decide to place them outside, make sure you bring them in each night and regularly inspect for new holes/mold. Depending on the weather, and how much sun is present, it will probably take about 3-4 days for them to dry completely.

Re-inspect again after the drying process, which might reveal cracks, blemishes, holes, or mold that wasn't present before. Remove any that aren't perfect. Store in bags in the freezer until you are ready to process and eat them.

The next step in the process is very important as it renders the acorn edible: removing the tannic acid. All oak trees produce acorns with differing degrees of tannic acid. White Oak acorns have relatively little, for example, while Red Oak acorns have a lot. But no matter which oak tree you harvest from, the acorns *will* have tannic acid, and they *will* need to be processed to make them edible. There are two ways of flushing the tannic acid from the acorns; cold-water and boiling.

Native Americans used the cold-water flushing method of leeching the tannic acid out by placing the acorns in a basket in a quickly moving stream or river for several days. Even through the outer hulls, the tannic acids, which are water soluble, would be removed, making the nuts safe to eat.

Pioneers, however, probably used the method that was a little more controllable: boiling. While boiling could remove some of the flavor of the acorn, it was also a far quicker process (though still takes a bit of time!), and one in which the settler could be sure that the goal of making the acorn fit to consume had been achieved. Here's how they did it:

- Have two large stock pots filled with cold water (make sure there is enough water to cover the acorns you will add, but don't add the acorns yet!).
- Turn on the heat under the first pot.
- While it is coming to the boil, crack and shell your acorns.
- Inspect the meat and discard any that have mold, blemishes, or larvae.
- Roughly chop your acorn nutmeat.
- When the water is boiling, add the chopped acorns and IMMEDIATELY turn off the heat, letting the acorns steep in the hot water for 30 minutes.
- Turn on the heat under the second pot of cold water.
- By the time 30 minutes has passed, the water in the first pot should have turned brown.
- Strain the acorns from the first pot and place them in the second pot of BOILING water.

- Turn that pot off IMMEDIATELY after adding the acorns and allow 30 more minutes of steeping time.
- (If you wish, you can save the brown water to use in tanning hides or other recipes.)
- Rinse the first pot and fill again with cold water and put back on the heat.
- After the second steeping, drain the acorns and taste a small piece.
- If they are still very bitter, repeat the steeping/draining process until they are almost free of bitterness.
- If only a very little bitterness remains, add 2 tablespoons of pickling or canning salt to your final pot of boiling water.
- When the salt is dissolved, add the chopped acorns to the boiling water for one final steep.
- Make sure to turn the pot off. . .too much boiling will make the acorns mushy.
- After the final 30 minutes of steeping, drain the acorns.

For coffee, you will now need to roast the acorns by drying in a low oven (cracking the door to let the moisture escape), then turning the oven up to about 400°F until brown and roasted, stirring often to prevent burning. Grind and use as you would regular coffee, though you will probably need to use a larger proportion of grounds to get a sufficiently strong brew.

Food Timeline quotes the following instructional from the Family Receipt Book (1819). It touts the medicinal benefits of acorn coffee, but it omits any directions for leaching the tannic acid out of the acorns. Whether that is because it was assumed that everyone knew to do that before using acorns, or whether they believed it unnecessary, I don't know, but it certainly isn't a step that should be missed.

Take sound a ripe acorns, peel off the shell or husk, divide the kernels, dry them gradually, and then roast them in a close vessel or roaster, keeping them continually stirring; in doing which special care must be taken that they be not burnt or roasted too much, both which would be hurtful. Take of these roasted acorns (ground like other coffee) half an ounce every other morning and evening, alone mixed with a dram of other coffee, and sweetened with sugar, or with or without milk. This receipt is recommended by a famous German physician, as a much esteemed, wholesome nourishing, strengthening nutriment for mankind; which, by its medicinal qualities, had been found to cure slimy obstructions in the viscera, and to remove nervous complaints when other medicines have failed. (Food Timeline, *Acorns*)

Over Roasted Barley

Another popular coffee substitute was over roasted barley. This is an old recipe, pulled from many difference sources, but the closest online version I found was at food.com:

- Add 1 cup of either pot or pearl barley to a strainer.
- Rinse well under cold water.
- Towel dry.
- Heat a heavy skillet (cast iron works perfectly) until a drop of water sizzles when plopped in.
- Add barley and stir constantly with a wooden spoon.
- Dry roast until it turns a light to medium brown.
- Remove from heat, cool and then grind.
- Roast the ground barley again until dark and fragrant, being very careful not to burn it!
- Use as you would regular coffee.

As with all substitutes, you'll have to play around with proportions to find the perfect grounds-to-water ratio for you, but start with the typical 2 tablespoons to 6 ounces of water ratio and adjust from there.

Dyspepsia Coffee

What is it? Well, dyspepsia is just a fancy name for indigestion, so we can surmise from the following recipe that this was a coffee blend meant either to cure indigestion or, perhaps, to prevent it:

Take a pint of corn meal and mix with molasses enough to wet it; put in a bake pan and brown the same as coffee. Put half meal and half coffee, which makes the coffee excellent. (Food Timeline, *Dyspepsia Coffee*)

COCOA

Cocoa has had quite a transformation from its first incarnation. The Mayan Indians are credited with first harvesting and using the cacao beans, though there seems to be evidence that the Oltecs had a grip on their cultivation and harvesting well before that. There is no doubt, however, that the Mayans were decidedly in love with the beans and were crucial in their spread.

Almost as soon as they discovered cacao, the Mayans began trading this treasure with the nearby (and decidedly more aggressive) Aztecs, and suddenly, those precious beans were a hot commodity. Used as gifts and in various celebrations and even as currency, cacao bean derived beverages were deemed 'the drink of the gods.'

But, frankly, this was NOT your grandmother's hot cocoa! With ingredients ranging from corn to chili peppers to wine and various herbs and spices, the first cacao based drinks were neither creamy nor sweet. By all accounts, they were room-temperature beverages using whole, crushed cacao beans in bitter, spicy combinations. A far cry from what we enjoy today!

By the early 1500's, the Spanish explorer, Hernan Cortez, got hold of the beans and established a plantation to grow them in Mexico. He didn't seem thrilled with the drink itself, but was determined to capitalize on the fact that the Indians used the beans as currency! After a year, Cortez brought cacao back to the King of Spain. The website The Nibble explains what happened next:

> [T]he Conquistadors found the recipe unpalatable, and when they brought the beans back to Spain to King Ferdinand and Queen Isabella, royal chefs promptly introduced ingredients to make it more palatable: sugar, rice, cinnamon, anise seed and black pepper. It was still a far cry from what most of us think of when we hear the words "drinking chocolate." (The Nibble, *Hot Chocolate History*)

37

For the next hundred years or so, the beans were largely a Spanish secret from the rest of Europe. To be honest, the lack of outside interest could be more from the fact that the actual drink wasn't too good than any subversive Spanish plot to keep it for themselves! The fact was, even with the marked improvements in ingredients, it was still made with water, usually not warm, and contained the whole cacao beans. However, there is some evidence that by the mid-1600's it was beginning to be mixed with milk:

> In 1645, Tomas Hurtado, who held a chair in theology at the University of Seville, judged that chocolate was a drink if made with water, but a food when milk or eggs were used in the preparation. By this we know that some chocolate was prepared with milk at least as early as the mid-17th century. (The Nibble, *Hot Chocolate History*)

Eventually, the secret got out and new recipes came flooding in. . .cocoa was getting closer and closer to what we now know and love. By the mid-to late1600's, snooty chocolate-houses started popping up amongst popular coffee-houses. Both catered to the elite, though tea was still the most expensive drink in town.

The biggest break in the transformation of the beverage finally came in 1828. Discovering a way to press out the cocoa butter from the cacao bean, a chemist from the Netherlands, Coenrad J. Van Houten, solved a huge problem and began a bit of a revolution. By removing a large portion of the fat content of the beans, the mass that was left could now be easily ground up into a fine powder, which mixed better with liquids. Before that, cacao beans were kind of ground and boiled and the fat had to be repeatedly skimmed off. Yum.

Van Houten took his idea one step further by adding a little alkaline salts to the powder, and the blending was even better! This

"Dutching" of the beans meant that not only was cocoa more accessible as a beverage, but it could also now be used in other recipes. Remember, up until this point, cocoa was strictly a beverage. From this point forward, however, solid forms of chocolate began to appear.

Here's a recipe using the bars of pressed drinking chocolate available in the late 1700's:

To Make Chocolate. Scrape four ounces of chocolate and pour a quart of boiling water upon it, mill it well with a chocolate mill and sweeten it to your taste. Give it a boil and let it stand all night, then mill it again very well. Boil it two minutes, then mill it till it will leave a froth upon the top of your cups. (Food Timeline, *Hot Chocolate*)

"Scraping" merely meant "grating" it, and "milling" simply meant mixing it very, very well. . .as close to whipping it as possible given the kitchen tools of the day. Without stick blenders, hand-mixers, or food processors, whisking as rapidly as possible to blend all of the ingredients and cocoa butter fats would have been the goal. It was a very similar process to modern homogenization of milk.

By the time the mid-1800's arrived, and due to both Van Houten's processing discovery and the Fry Brothers 1847 invention of the chocolate bar, there emerged two distinct products: cocoa powder and chocolate that you drank. Cocoa had a richer and deeper chocolate flavor. Drinking chocolate was smoother and creamier.

Manufacturers then and now seem to be confused about which is which, at least when they label and advertise. Cocoa should, technically, refer to the powder of the cacao bean after much of the cocoa butter is pressed out. Hot chocolate is a beverage that is made from adding pellets or shavings of chocolate to heated milk or water. Both can produce a delicious chocolately beverage. The pioneers certainly realized this!

The amount of cocoa retained for home consumption in 1860 was only 1,181,054 pounds; in 1885 it was 8,426,787. (Food Timeline, *Cocoa*)

That, my friends, is a LOT of hot cocoa! Or hot chocolate! Or, well, whatever you want to call it!

Here's a recipe based on one from *Housekeeping in Old Virginia* (1879), edited by Marion Cabell Tyree:

Ingredients:

- Baker's chocolate bar, one ounce
- 1 pint Boiling water
- 1 pint Milk
- Sugar to taste

Method:

- Scrape (finely grate) chocolate bar.
- Add chocolate to milk and water in a heavy pot or sauce-pan.
- Boil for ten minutes.
- Mill (whip it) until well mixed and frothy.

But if you're VERY adventurous, how about this one found on the Jane Austen's World website:

The first recipe for a chocolate drink was published in Spain in 1644 by Antonio Colmenero de Ledesma in his book, *A Curious Treatise of the Nature and Quality of Chocolate*. The spices included hot chiles, and the recipe goes as follows:

- 100 cacao beans
- 2 chiles (black pepper may be substituted)
- A handful of anise
- "Ear flower"
- 1 vanilla pod
- 2 ounces cinnamon
- 12 almonds or hazelnuts
- pound sugar
- Achiote (annatto seeds) to taste

All of these ingredients were boiled together and then frothed with a molinillo, the traditional Aztec carved wooden tool. The achiote was used to redden the color of the drink.

HOT MILK

Cattle were first brought to the United States in the 1600s by some of the earliest colonists. Prior to the American Revolution, most of the dairy products were consumed on the farm where they were produced. By about 1790, population centers such as Boston, New York, and Philadelphia had grown sufficiently to become an attractive market for larger-scale dairy operations. To meet the increased demand, farmers began importing breeds of cattle that were better suited for milk production. The first Holstein-Friesens were imported in 1795, the first Ayrshires in 1822, and the first Guernseys in 1830. (How Products Are Made)

Just as comforting then as it is now, a steaming cup of milk hasn't changed much in the last two hundred years. Though pioneers usually saved limited milk supplies for the making of butter and cheese, when production was high, or in wealthier families with milk (or money!) to spare, it was back on the menu. As better breeds of milch cows were imported and bred, milk production for the home farm, as well as for sale, increased. Larger quantities of milk meant the luxury to explore a wider variety of uses. Warm milk was one of those uses.

Because it was easy to digest for most people, hot milk was a soothing drink that was deemed suitable for both children and the elderly, as well as adults and the infirm. It was warmed and consumed plain, or flavored exactly as we do now. . .with gratings of nutmeg, cinnamon, and perhaps a little sugar or honey.

Here is a simple recipe:

Hot Milk

Ingredients:

- Milk (6-8 ounces per serving)
- Cinnamon (1/4 teaspoon ground or 1 inch piece of cinnamon bark per serving)
- OR, Nutmeg (1/8 teaspoon ground per serving)
- Sugar or honey to taste

Method:

- In clean saucepan, bring milk and cinnamon or nutmeg up almost to scalding.
- If you used cinnamon bark, remove it.
- Stir in sugar or honey to taste.
- Whip quickly for a little froth on top, if desired.
- Pour into mugs.
- Top with a sprinkle more of cinnamon or nutmeg, if desired.
- Serve immediately.

MULLED CIDER (NON-ALCOHOLIC)

Cider, as we know it today, is the fresh pressed juice of apples. It distinguishes itself from apple juice by being unfiltered and/or unpasteurized. It's sweet, fresh, and, because it's unprocessed, goes off very quickly. It's a swift jump from fresh cider to fermented (alcoholic) cider to vinegar under the right conditions, too, so storage is pretty important if you aren't trying to be a brewery or a vinegar factory.

Interestingly, before the publication of the *Little House on the Prairie* books, most references to cider were as an alcoholic beverage. Strictly grown as a crop to make hard (or alcoholic) cider, apples had been cultivated for centuries before they ever made it to American shores. Hard cider was easy to store and far safer than dodgy British drinking water supplies.

An interesting note:

Cider, a term with two meanings. In N. America since Prohibition it refers to unfermented, unpasteurized, and usually unfiltered apple juice. . .Alcoholic cider is now described as 'hard' cider. . .In Britain, cider is an alcoholic drink, for which special cider apples are used. (Davidson, p. 190)

So why, then, did Laura Ingalls Wilder mention cider in her book "Farmer Boy" as a family beverage drunk cozily each night after dinner? I'm not sure. There are many period references to children drinking hard cider, but precious little about cider as the family-friendly fresh juice of an apple that must be pressed and drunk quickly before fermentation occurs. The website WineIntro explains:

Cider always had alcohol in it. Especially in New England, cider was an immensely popular drink with the pilgrims and was drunk at meals by everyone, including children. Even clergymen, while denouncing 'harder spirits', would drink cider as a matter of course. (Shea)

The George Mason University Website confirms:

John Hull Brown reports that from the early 18th century to 1825 even children drank hard cider with breakfast and dinner. (GMU)

So what did Laura mean when she wrote about Almanzo's family drinking cider each night? Was the beverage she described innocently non-alcoholic, which would have been highly unusual in the mid 1800's, or was it 'hard' cider that was simply a culturally acceptable beverage for children? The concept is intriguing. Given the fact that it was stored down cellar in barrels, it was most likely alcoholic! Freshly made cider would not have stored that long in an innocent state!

Either way, cider could be consumed chilled or warmed. We'll look at alcoholic versions of cider later, but for now, we're sticking with a G-rated family recipe for delicious mulled cider!

Mulled Cider (Non-alcoholic)

Ingredients/Equipment:

- 48 ounces Freshly Pressed Apple Cider (or Apple Juice if you prefer)
- 16 ounces Water
- 2 large Cinnamon sticks
- ½ small Nutmeg, grated
- ½ tablespoon Cloves
- Juice and zest of one large Orange
- Heavy bottomed Stockpot
- Muslin or Cheesecloth square
- Butcher's String to tie cloth

- ¼ teaspoon Mace, if desired
- Sugar to taste, if desired

Method:

- Tie spices and orange peel in square of cloth.
- Boil water and place cloth in water to steep for 15 minutes.
- Add water, cloth, and apple cider to saucepan.
- Heat to a low simmer and cook for 15 minutes.
- Just before serving, add orange juice and taste.
- Add sugar if needed.
- Remove and discard spices and serve immediately.
- Make 8 servings.

Interesting Fact: New Hampshire adopted Apple Cider as its state drink in 2010! I wonder if it's the hard or non-alcoholic version??

PART 2:

Cold

COLD DRINKS

Without refrigeration, cold drinks were not a particularly regular part of a settler's diet during warm spring and summer months. Unless a pioneer was established and prosperous, the likelihood that he had an ice house in which to store beverages or retrieve refreshing slivers of ice to make them was not particularly high.

So, "cold drinks" were far more likely to be room temperature or, if he was lucky, slightly cool (as in water from a well or cool milk stored in a cellar). For the purpose of this book, "cold drinks" are those which the settlers did not heat and were intended to refresh and restore on a warm summer's day.

LEMONADE

Throughout period literature, references are made to lemonade. Usually reserved for special occasions, like Fourth of July Celebrations or church picnics, it was regarded as a very rare and delicious treat, especially when made in a barrel with cool water and plenty of lemons and sugar were put in. When did lemons make their first American appearance? Wikipedia explains:

> The lemon was introduced to the Americas in 1493 when Christopher Columbus brought lemon seeds to Hispaniola on his voyages. Spanish conquest throughout the New World helped spread lemon seeds. It was mainly used as an ornamental plant and for medicine. In the 19th century, lemons were increasingly planted in Florida and California. (Wikipedia, *Lemon*)

Because lemons were being grown on American soil by the 1800's, prices would have been less than the previously imported varieties, but to a settler on the open prairie, they would have still been a rare and costly treat. MyLittlePrairieHome.com has a great recipe:

Prairie Lemonade

Ingredients:

- 8 lemons, juiced
- 1 cup of sugar (white or the pioneer version: light brown)
- 5 cups of water, divided
- Ice, if so desired
- Large pitcher
- Long wooden spoon

Method:

- Mix one cup of very warm water with the sugar. Stir until the sugar is dissolved.
- Add the rest of the water, which should be very cold, stirring well.
- Add the juice of the lemons, either fully strained (if you don't like pulp!) or just ensuring the seeds are removed.
- Taste to adjust and pour over glasses filled with ice to serve.

Note: lemons come in all different sizes and juice content and natural sweetness. Because of this, these proportions are just a guideline. If you like a more lemony drink, add more. If the final product is too sour, add sugar. If it is too strong, dilute with a little more water. The pioneers rarely measured much . . . they went by sight and taste and feel! (My Little Prairie Home, *Lemonade*)

Interesting Fact: Lemon Flavoring was sometimes used as a substitute for real lemon juice when making beverages. It could be purchased at most general stores, or, if you were lucky enough to get your hand on some lemons, it could be made at home. Add ½ cup of liquor (whiskey, rum, or brandy) to the finely chopped zest (yellow bit of the peel) of one lemon. Store in a tightly corked jar (in a cool, dark place). Shake well every day or two. At the end of three weeks, strain out the zest and your lemon flavoring is ready for use!

PIONEER (MOCK) LEMONADE

Between the significant cost of real lemons and the infrequency of trips to town, real lemonade was likely rare for the pioneers. But that sure didn't stop them! They simply used what they had to concoct a makeshift version of the popular beverage: Pioneer Lemonade.

Undeniably an acquired taste, Pioneer Lemonade did have several things going for it: It was cheap, easy to make, and the ingredients were usually at hand. MyLittlePrairieHome.com has the recipe:

Ingredients:

- ½ cup Apple Cider Vinegar
- 6 cups of water
- ½-¾ cup of sugar

Method:

- Mix together until sugar is dissolved.
- Adjust to taste (dilute more with water, add more sugar, add more vinegar, etc.).
- Enjoy!

ICED TEA

I was a little surprised to discover that Iced Tea has been around since at least the 1850's. As we've already noted, ice wasn't particularly accessible to the general masses. (Except in winter, of course, when a cooling beverage was unlikely to be desired.) So discovering that it existed at all, let alone became a raging favorite by the 1870's was certainly surprising.

In *Craig Claiborne's The New York Times Food Encyclopedia*, the author wrote "Iced tea appeared in the United States, the creation of some anonymous individual, prior to the Civil War". In 1860 a writer for Horace Greely's Tribune, Solon Robinson, published a small volume How to Live: "Last summer we got in the habit of taking the tea iced, and really thought it better than when hot. By 1871 the new beverage competed with iced milk, and iced water on hot summer days at the Fifth Avenue Hotel. In New York...By 1878, travelers found iced tea for sale on the Rock Island Railroad and a popular beverage in Sidney, Nebraska. Cookbooks began to offer recipes for iced tea and in 1886 Senators in their Washington offices were said to have had large coolers of it to mitigate the force of the weather." (Reddit: AskHistorians)

Exactly when the custom of drinking iced tea began is unknown, but it dates back at least to the 1860s, if not long before. A hot drink in vogue in the 1870s, tea a la Russe, made with sugar and sliced lemons, was also enjoyed cold. Iced tea was also available in the 1870s in hotels and on railroads. (Tea Beyond)

Iced Tea Recipe

- Begin by making hot tea.

Ingredients/Equipment:

- One generous teaspoon of loose leaf tea per cup, plus one for the pot if you are making at least 6 cups of tea
- Fresh water, preferably artesian spring rather than tap, freshly boiled, 6 ounces per cup desired
- Pot
- Tea strainer
- Tea cozy or clean towel

Method:

- Warm your pot by adding very hot water and letting it stand for five minutes.
- Drain water and add tea leaves to pot.
- Pour in water that had been brought to a vigorous boil, then rested for one minute.
- Do not stir the tea leaves.
- Place the lid on the pot and wrap in a cozy or towel.
- When tea is prepared, let it cool to room temperature.
- Strain into glasses filled with ice.
- Add sugar to taste, and slices of lemon, if desired.

SWITCHEL

Pa told Laura to drink first but not too much. Nothing was ever so good as that cool wetness going down her throat. At the taste of it she stopped in surprise and Carrie clapped her hands and cried out, laughing, "Don't tell, Laura, don't tell till Pa tastes it!" (Wilder, *The Long Winter*)

The surprise Ma sent to Laura and Pa on Laura's first day of making hay was *switchel*. She called it 'ginger water,' and there are a number of other names for the same basic drink: Swanky, Haymaker's Punch, Harvest Drink and Harvest Beer. The central ingredients called for water, vinegar, molasses, and ginger, though housewives often added their own secret ingredients to improve the taste. Some farmers believed that farmhands worked better warmed up than cooled down and added rum to the basic mix to accomplish just that.

Ma's version was definitely non-alcoholic. She "sweetened the cool well-water with sugar, flavored it with vinegar, and put in plenty of ginger to warm their stomachs so that they could drink till they were not thirsty." (*Ibid.*) The idea was that the vinegar and ginger would prevent stomach cramps, molasses provided energy and flavor, and the water washed the dust from workers throats.

Made primarily during haymaking time, switchel was an important, thirst-quenching part of harvest.

Many of the large New England hayfields have disappeared; so has the switchel, which is now merely a name. Switchel was a mixture of molasses, ginger, water and a dash of vinegar, contained in a brown jug cached under the shade of a bunch of alders or partly submerged in a spring hole. On a hot day when men were mowing, raking, or pitching hay, frequent trips were made to the switchel jug. Dusty throats needed something to wash away the hayseed, and switchel was the answer. It was consumed in quantities. The coldness of the water was tempered by the molasses, while the ginger and vinegar prevented cramps. (Food Timeline, *Switchel*)

Harvest Drink. Mix with five gallons of good water, half a gallon of molasses, one quart of vinegar, and two ounces of powdered ginger. This will make not only a very pleasant beverage, but one highly invigorating and healthful. (Bradley)

Ingredients:

- 2 Quarts Cold Water
- ½ cup Apple Cider Vinegar
- ¼ cup Molasses
- ½ cup Brown Sugar
- 2 teaspoons ground Ginger

Method:

- Mix all ingredients until sugar is dissolved and serve

Note: Switchel can be made with any combination of molasses/honey/sugar, so long as it adds up to ¾ of a cup of sweetener. Some people unaccustomed to the strong flavors prefer to thin this out with more water or add more sugar to taste.

MILK

Though Mary Ingalls certainly seemed to enjoy a cold, creamy glass of Ma's milk, the fact is, most settlers did not drink milk on a regular basis. Milk is highly perishable, especially in typical pioneer conditions, so it was usually reserved for making butter and cheese, which had a much longer shelf life.

When milk was plentiful, however, during the height of summer or if the family was prosperous enough to have more than one cow, fresh, creamy milk was certainly an enjoyable addition to any meal. For the most part, settlers had to do without a number of the conveniences and niceties that their neighbors in cities enjoyed. But milk was one luxury that only the very rich and the farmer shared. By the time milk could be transported from farms into the cities, it would have gone bad. So, most city dwellers, except those who were wealthy, had to do without.

To prepare milk for drinking, several things had to happen:

- First, it was strained soon after milking and placed in wide, shallow milk pans. Straining removed any debris that found its way into the pail during milking.

- Left undisturbed overnight, the cream would rise to the top and would then be skimmed to use as is or, more likely, to be made into butter.

- The remaining milk would then be poured into jugs or milk cans and stored either 'down cellar' or in a milk house, which was a small building built over a stream. Being cool, both a milk house and a cellar would slightly prolong the lifespan of fresh milk, but not by much. Most was used in cooking, the making of fermented milk products (like clabbered milk), or in the making of cheese.

BUTTERMILK

The buttermilk of today is a far cry from what the settlers had. What you will now find in stores is a thick, creamy, tangy beverage that is really a cultured form of milk. When the settlers spoke of traditional buttermilk, they were meaning the thin, watery, grayish liquid left over from the process of making butter. Very different thing!

Despite technically being a waste product, buttermilk was historically highly prized. Long considered a huge 'perk' for shepherds and dairy maids, buttermilk was considered as delicious as it was nutritious. In fact, "in the days when the peasantry of Ireland subsisted on potatoes, buttermilk was what they washed them down with." (Ayto, *Buttermilk*)

Along with regular milk, and just as perishable, it was another healthy benefit enjoyed by the farmer that city-dwellers simply had no access to.

How do you get it? Simple! You make butter!

The process of making butter separates the fat globules from the liquid and milk solids in cream. What is left looks nothing like milk, nor like modern cultured buttermilk, but it is remarkably healthy since most of the fat is removed. Just like milk, however, buttermilk must be used either as a drink or in cooking quickly after being made as fermentation begins to occur very shortly after milk leaves the cow.

Fresh buttermilk is light and almost watery. It has a very mild tangy taste and is quite refreshing. Being that there is no modern equivalent for it, though, it might take a little getting used to. Here is how to make your own (as well as some fantastic butter as a by-product!).

Ingredients:

- One pint heavy cream (at least 30% butterfat)

Method:

- Set the cream, in its original container, on the counter at room temperature for about 4-5 hours. This will help it to thicken and slightly sour the cream
- Put the cream back in the fridge for an hour to re-chill.
- For churning, there are two methods to try: one requires time and muscle, the other a mixer

If you go with the time and muscle option:

- Pour your cream into a large mason jar with a tight lid. Make sure that you fill it no more than ½ to ⅔ of the way, so you have some expansion room.
- Start shaking the jar vigorously (holding carefully so it doesn't go flying!)
- Eventually, the cream will start to thicken into whipped cream. Keep going.
- Just before the cream breaks into butter and buttermilk, it will be so thick in the jar that it doesn't feel like anything is moving or happening. Get your second wind and keep at it.
- You'll know that the butter has been made when you see the cream divided into floating little globules of butter and a watery liquid. Keep shaking for a minute or two more to ensure that all the cream is separated.
- Strain buttermilk away from the butter, making sure to save it. (If you don't want to drink it, it's perfect for pancakes or biscuits or other baking).
- So that the butter doesn't go to waste, rinse it under very cold water until the water runs clear.
- Place in a cold bowl and cover with ice cold water.
- Using either butter paddles or wooden spoons, or even your own hands if you are quick enough and don't mind the icy

water, knead the butter, pushing it up against the sides of the bowl, to release any buttermilk still trapped inside the butter. If you leave it, the butter solids will soon go sour and your butter will have an 'off' taste!

- When the water gets cloudy, pour it off and cover again with icy water.
- Repeat the kneading/rinsing until no cloudiness appears in the water no matter how hard you knead the butter.
- When the butter is completely free of milk solids, drain well and press out as much water as you can with wooden spoons or butter paddles. (your hands will melt the butter at this stage!)
- Add salt, starting at ½ teaspoon and mix well. Taste and add more salt if you like. Salt adds flavor and is also a pre-servative.

If you're going with the easier, quicker, and obviously more modern method:

- Pour your cream into your standing mixer in the largest bowl possible.
- Beat on medium high.
- After your cream gets very stiff, it will break into butter and buttermilk just like in the jar method.
- Keep beating for a minute or two until you are sure that all the cream is separated.
- Strain buttermilk from the butter, making sure to save it.
- Rinse butter under very cold water until the it runs clear.
- Return to your mixing bowl and cover with ice cold water.
- With your beaters on low, mix the butter and water until it gets cloudy with the remaining buttermilk.

- When the water gets cloudy, pour it off and cover butter again with icy water.
- Repeat the mixing/rinsing until absolutely no cloudiness appears in the water no matter how much you mix the butter.
- When the butter is completely free of milk solids, drain well and press out as much water as you can with wooden spoons or butter paddles. (your hands will melt the butter at this stage!)

When the butter making process is done, place your reserved buttermilk in the fridge to get ice-cold. You can drink it as-is, or, if you need a more modern application to please your palate, mix into a smoothie, or use in any baking or pancake recipe in place of regular milk.

Why did the settlers drink buttermilk? First, it was considered a tasty treat. Remember that their palates were often geared toward a much more sour diet. . .which included large amounts of vinegar, brined meats and sourdough breads, etc. More than that, however, it was recognized as being quite healthy. Given their relatively limited diets, a wise pioneer never missed an opportunity to consume nutritious foods. This is how Wikipedia describes the benefits of traditional buttermilk:

Buttermilk prepared in the traditional way is considered beneficial to health as it contains probiotic microbes and is sometimes referred to as 'Grandma's probiotic.' It is also soothing to stomach and skin. The fat content of buttermilk is far lower than milk or curd as fat is removed during churning. The probiotic nature of buttermilk is beneficial to the gut and improves immunity when taken regularly. (Wikipedia, *Buttermilk*)

WHEY

Whey is similar to traditional buttermilk in that it is actually a by-product of another dairy process: cheese making. Just like buttermilk is the thin liquid left over when butterfat is removed from milk during the making of butter, whey is the thin liquid left over when rennet is added to milk and curds of cheese are formed.

Whey contains a lot of protein and is available in health food stores as both a drink and a supplement. Because it is also an acquired taste, however, many people choose to add it to smoothies or mix with other beverages. There are two kinds of whey:

> *Sweet whey* is manufactured during the making of rennet types of hard cheese like cheddar or Swiss cheese. *Acid whey* (also known as "sour whey") is a by-product produced during the making of acid types of dairy products such as cottage cheese or strained yogurt. (Wikipedia, *Whey*)

For those in America in the 1800's, whey would have either been drunk immediately after cheese-making or mixed in with animal feed to boost nutrition. Not a lot of settlers realized that other things could be made from whey. Because it looks so thin and watery, it is easy to be unaware that it still contains a lot of milk solids. Other parts of the world used whey to make ricotta cheese, brown cheeses, and many other products, but the pioneers most likely would not have known to do that.

> Throughout history, whey was a popular drink in inns and coffee houses. When Joseph Priestley was at college at Daventry Academy 1752–1755, he records that, during the morning of Wednesday 22 May 1754, he "went with a large company to drink whey." This was probably 'sack whey' or 'wine whey.' (*Ibid.*)

GINGER BEER/GINGER ALE

In an age where some children probably did drink mildly alcoholic beverages (think: Almanzo's cider!), it's no surprise that Ginger Beer actually began its life as a low-alcohol concoction. Sort of a bridge between hard liquor and sodas, if you will. Given the fairly minor alcohol content and the swift transition to a non-alcoholic version (Ginger Ale), we've included it in this section, rather than the section on alcoholic beverages. But only by a hair's breadth! Consider this brief history from the website RestorationShed.com:

> By the first century AD traders had brought the root to the Mediterranean and by the Middle Ages, ginger was coveted throughout Europe. It was also very expensive: one pound of ginger would get you a live sheep. In the sixteenth century, Henry VIII was recommending it as remedy for the plague while his daughter, Queen Elizabeth, invented what now we call the gingerbread man.
>
> Flash forward to the nineteenth century, when ginger ale's old brother, ginger beer, was first made. Who knows whether the inventor was curious, drunk, or merely unsatisfied with his beer, but powdered ginger was added to a beer and stirred with a hot poker, creating "ginger beer". Soon thousands of local taverns and breweries across the United Kingdom, Canada, and the US were brewing up their own varieties. Some had an alcohol content of up to 11%.
>
> In 1852, an unfermented, non-alcoholic version of ginger beer was first made for children and non-drinkers by Dr. Cantrell in Belfast, Ireland, a well-known manufacturer of aerated and mineral waters. He called it "ginger ale" and the concoction tasted more intensely like ginger than the ginger-flavored

beers of the day. The good doctor described it as "sparkling and clear as the choicest champagne, as having a most agreeable odour, perfectly free from any intoxicating quality, and yet eminently warming and invigorating, pleasant to the taste and pleasant to look at." (Restoration Shed)

Here are several recipes from period sources:

To Make Ginger Beer. To every gallon of spring water add one ounce of sliced white ginger, one pound of common loaf sugar, and two ounces of lemon juice, or three large tablespoonfuls; boil it near an hour, and take off the scum; then run it through a hair sieve into a tub, and when cool, (viz. 70°) add yeast in proportion of half a pint to nine gallons; keep it in a temperate situation two days, during which it may be stirred six or eight times; then put it into a cask, which must be kept full, and the yeast taken off at the bung-hole with a spoon. In a fortnight add half a pint of fining (isinglass picked and steeped in beer) to nine gallons, which will, if it has been properly fermented, clear it by ascent. The cask must be kept full, and the rising particles taken off at the bung-hole. When fine (which may be expected in twenty-four hours) bottle it, cork it well, and in summer it will be ripe and fit to drink in a fortnight. (Rundell)

Beer, Ginger. For a ten-gallon cask, eleven gallons of water, fourteen pounds of sugar, the juice of eighteen lemons, and one pound of ginger are allowed; the sugar and water are boiled with the whites of eight eggs, and well skimmed; just before coming to the boiling point, the ginger, which must be bruised, is then added, and boiled for twenty minutes; when cold, the clear part is put into the cask, together with the lemon-juice and two spoonfuls of yeast; when it has fermented for three or four days, it is fined, bunged up, and in a fortnight bottled. It may be made without the fruit. (Lee)

"**Beer, Ginger, Quickly Made.** A gallon of boiling water is poured over three-quarters of a pound of loaf sugar, one ounce and a quarter of ginger, and the peel of one lemon; when milk-warm, the juice of the lemon and a spoonful of yeast are added. It should be made in the evening, and bottled next morning, in half-pint stone bottles, and the cork tied down with twine." (*Ibid.*)

Ginger beer is made in the following proportions:--One cup of ginger, one pint of molasses, one pail and a half of water, and a cup of lively yeast. Most people scald the ginger in half a pail of water, and then fill it up with a pailful of cold; but in very hot weather some people stir it up cold. Yeast must not be put in till it is cold, or nearly cold. If not to be drank within twenty-four hours, it must be bottled as soon as it works. (Child)

Ginger Beer.--Break up a pound and a half of loaf-sugar, and mix it with three ounces of strong white ginger, and the grated peel of two lemons. Put these ingredients into a large stone jar, and pour over them two gallons of boiling water. When it becomes milkwarm strain it, and add the juice of the lemons and two large table-spoonfuls of strong yeast. Make this beer in the evening and let it stand all night. Next morning bottle it in a little half pint stone bottles, tying down the corks with twine. (Leslie)

Ginger Drink. Ginger, as a rule, agrees with the stomach, especially in warm weather. Dissolve two and three-quarter pounds of sugar in two gallons of soft water; then add the well-beaten whites of three eggs and two ounces of Jamaica ginger. It is well to moisten the ginger in a little cold water before adding it to the whole amount of water. Bring all this slowly to boiling point, skim, and stand aside to cool. When cold add the juice of one large lemon and two tablespoonfuls of yeast, or a quarter of a compresed cake dissolved. Fill it into bottles, cork tightly, and tie the corks down. Stand the bottles in a cool place for ten days, and they are ready for use. (*Medical Era*)

ROOT BEER

Just like Ginger Beer, the origins of Root Beer lie with small beer. Small beer was low-alcohol, usually made at home, and far less potent than commercially available versions. Because small beer was a home-brew, it was often produced from an unusual array of ingredients, including the roots of medicinal plants, ginger, and, popularly, spruce. By the mid 1800's, soft drinks (made from flavored seltzer waters and soda) were starting to appear on the market, typically touted as 'health food products.' This was the market Root Beer fits into.

Though it wasn't produced commercially until about 1876, it had been around for decades at that point. According to the *Oxford English Dictionary* (2nd edition), a print reference to "root beer" was published in 1843. Furthermore, author Nathaniel Hawthorne mentions both "root beer" and "ginger beer" in his book *House of Seven Gables*, which was published in 1851.

"**Root Beer**: For each gallon of water to be used, take hops, burdock, yellow dock, sarsaparilla, dandelion, and spikenard roots, bruised, of each 1/2 oz., bruised, boil about 20 minutes, and strain while hot, add 8 or 10 drops of oils of spruce and sassafras mixed in equal proportions, when cool enough not to scald your hand, put in 2 or 3 table-spoonfuls of yeast; molasses 2/3 of a pint, or white sugar 1/2 lb. gives it about the right sweetness. Keep these proportions for as many gallons as you wish to make. You can use more or less of the roots to suit your taste after trying it; it is best to get the dry roots, or dig them and let them get dry, and of course you can add any other root known to possess medicinal properties desired in the beer. After all is mixed, let it stand in a jar with a cloth thrown over it, to work about two hours, then bottle and set in a cool place. This is a nice way to take *Alteratives*, without taking *Medicine*. (Chase)

There is a brilliant project by Michigan State University called *Feeding America: The Historic American Cookbook Project.* Its purpose was to create an online collection of important and influential late 18th through early 20th century cookbooks. They are digitally scanned and available to view online.

From that awesome site, here is a recipe for Spruce Beer (which is root beer) taken from *American Cookery* by Amelia Simmons [Hartford: Printed for Simeon Butler, Northampton, (1798)]. This is a particularly important cookbook in American history as it was the first cookbook written by an American for Americans. . .not merely a re-print of British publications:

> *For brewing Spruce Beer*: Take four ounces of hops, let them boil half an hour in one gallon of water, strain the hop water then add sixteen gallons of warm water, two gallons of molasses, eight ounces of essence of spruce, dissolved in one quart of water, put it in a clean cask, then shake it well together, add half a pint of emptins, then let it stand and work one week, if very warm weather less time will do, when it is drawn off to bottle, add one spoonful of molasses to every bottle. (Simmons)

(What are "Emptins?" According to lexic.us it's either a liquid leavening, the sediment of beer or cider, or the yeast obtained from the remains of the brewing process!)

Also from the MSU project, this time from the cookbook *The Virginia House-wife*, written by Mary Randolph:

> **Spruce Beer**: Boil a handful of hops, and twice as much of the chippings of sassafras root, in ten gallons of water; strain it, and pour in, while hot, one gallon of molasses, two spoonsful of the essence of spruce, two spoonsful of powdered ginger,

and one of pounded allspice; put it in a cask—when sufficiently cold, add half a pint of good yeast; stir it well, stop it close, and when fermented and clear, bottle and cork it tight. (Randolph, p. 175)

Before setting foot on American shores, the making of root-based beers were not uncommon. The New World offered new flavors however:

When colonists arrived in North America, they found new varieties of the traditional spruce and birch for their beers, but discovered Native Americans using such novel flavorings as the roots of sarsaparilla (Smilax ornata) and sassafras (Sassafras albidum) as well. Both of these were similar to spruce and birch in taste, and the colonists soon learned to use them in their small beer, often with molasses as a sweetener and fermenting agent. (Food Timeline, *Rootbeer*)

PART 3:

Alcohol

ALCOHOLIC BEVERAGES

"[T]he period from the 1790s to the early 1830s was probably the heaviest drinking era in the nation's history." Mean absolute alcohol intake rose from 5.8 gallons in 1790 (people aged 15 or older) to 7.1 gallons per year in 1810; it held at that level, "with minor fluctuations", until "at least 1830." Samuel Dexter noted in 1814 that "the quantity of ardent spirits… surpasses belief." While he was the president of the Massachusetts Society for the Suppression of Intemperance, his data "closely approximate modern consumption estimates". By 1800, about half the absolute alcohol consumed was distilled liquor. It was well over half by 1810. In 1830, 4.3 gallons were hard liquor and 2.8 were beer, cider, or wine. (Hoboes.com)

By the mid nineteenth century, alcohol had thankfully had its heyday. As early colonists had moved from beer and ale and wine toward more potent spirits, and then learned the devastating consequences, a huge backlash against the 'evils of alcohol' emerged. Temperance movements in all states were active and beginning to be successful on a number of fronts, from local ordinances up through legislature.

Prominent political and medical figures documented the rampant damage of hard liquor, and America was beginning to listen. The website hoboes.com explains:

On June 2, 1851, a Maine law was signed "prohibiting the sale of beverage alcohol in the state." They had tried a similar provision in 1846, but it had been mild, "striking no terror to the hearts of the liquor dealers," as one temperance worker put it. The 1851 version "provided for the destruction of any liquor confiscated after the bill became law." It was America's first statewide prohibition statute. "All eyes were at once turned to

Maine," an antiliquor crusader said. But actually, they were on one city: Portland. Portland's mayor was Neal Dow, the "Prophet of Prohibition", and the "Father of the Maine Law", as he was known in his time. He issued an ultimatum: liquor dealers had sixty days to get their stocks out of town. . . . By 1855, twelve additional states and two Canadian provinces enacted Maine Laws of their own. The "general outlook for temperance appeared bright." (*Ibid.*)

This didn't eradicate liquor, however. . .not by a long shot! It did, however, limit its commercial availability and social acceptance to some degree. However, as much of the production of alcohol was home-based, many settlers took their knowledge, ability, and desire to produce and consume alcohol right along with them as they headed off to the west.

So what were the 'evil spirits' available to the settlers? Here's a partial list, with a brief definition and overview of the more popular spirits:

Wine:	Fermented Grapes
Beer:	Made from water, yeast, malted barley and hops.
Ale:	One of two main categories of beer. It's fermented at a high temperature and has a richer, more aggressive 'hoppy' taste.
Lager:	The second of two main categories of beer. Fermented at a much cooler temperature than ale, it is smoother and more mild.
Mead:	Fermented from honey.
Sack:	A fortified Spanish wine.
Applejack:	Brandy distilled from hard apple cider.
Cider:	An alcoholic beverage made from the fermented juice of pressed apples.

Perry: Hard Apple Cider made with either a mix of apples and pears or straight pears.

Cider could be made from apples mixed with pears, but if the drink was prepared largely or entirely of pears, it was usually called perry...Both cider and perry helped to save the grain for brewing, as did other country drinks. (Food Timeline, *Cider: How old is cider?*)

Gin: Grain spirits flavored with juniper berries.
Whiskey: Distilled from grains such as rye, barley or corn.
Bourbon: Corn whiskey aged in oak barrels.
Rum: Made from molasses or sugar cane, popular in the 1700s, but edged out by whiskey in the 1800's,

As settlements spread West in the 18th century, grain whiskeys began to compete with rum, which was too bulky and expensive to ship far inland. "Grain was plentiful—much more was harvested than farmers could eat or sell as food—and a single bushel of surplus corn, for example, yielded three gallons of whiskey….." (Hoboes.com)

Obviously, there were numerous variations of all of these general categories and a few others that didn't make the list. By the middle of the 18th century, pretty much no respectable woman would be caught drinking any of these beverages straight. However, there was still some respectability when used sparingly in other drinks.

Though contemporary palates are familiar with the concept and flavors of beverages made with cream, eggs and alcohol through modern day eggnog, there were actually a whole family of similar dessert beverages popular in the period: Sack Posset, Syllabub and our familiar Eggnog. Egg Caudle joins this crew, though it does not contain dairy.

> Rich and creamy dessert drinks, such as eggnog and syllabub, reflect the English heritage in America, especially in the South. In England posset was a hot drink in which the white and yolk of eggs were whipped with ale, cider, or wine. Americans adapted English recipes to produce a variety of milk-based drinks that combined rum, brandy, or whiskey with cream. The first written reference to eggnog was an account of a February 1796 breakfast at the City Tavern in Philadelphia. Beginning in 1839 American cookbooks included recipes for cold eggnogs of cream, sugar, and eggs combined with brandy, rum, bourbon, or sherry, sprinkled with nutmeg. Southerners enjoyed a mix of peach brandy, rum, and whiskey. (Smith, Andrew, p. 205)

So, we've got a lot of liquor, um, ground to cover!

SACK POSSET

They were a warming concoction of hot milk mixed with hot beer, sherry, etc., sugar, and various spices, excellent for keeping the cold at bay in the days before central heating, and no doubt effective as a nightcap too. (Food Timeline, *Egg nog: What is Posset?*)

Sounds rather yummy, doesn't it?!?! Erm. . .notsomuch. But wait. . .it gets worse!

Not only was this a drink made from either milk or cream and hot alcohol, but the milk was slightly curdled from the acid in the wine, ale, or citrus juice as a bonus. Many versions were thickened with eggs and some were so thick they were called 'eating possets' rather than possets meant for drinking. I can't imagine why these went out of fashion! Curdled milky eggy alcohol drinks? *Yes, please*!

Posset in its earliest medieval form was a drink made from milk lightly curdled by adding an acid liquid such as wine, ale, citrus juice to it. It was sweetened and often spiced. (Davidson, p. 644)

The website FoodTimeline.org offers some intriguing recipes at http://www.foodtimeline.org/christmasfood.html#posset:

My Lord of Carlisle's Sack-posset Take a Pottle of Cream, and boil in it a little whole Cinnamon, and three or four flakes of Mace. To this proportion of Cream put in eighteen yolks of Eggs, and eight of the whites; a pint of Sack; beat your Eggs very well, and then mingle them with your Sack. Put in three quarters of a pound of Sugar into the Wine and Eggs with a Nutmeg grated, and a little beaten Cinnamon; set the basin on the fire with the wine and Eggs, and let it be hot. Then put in the Cream boyling from the fire, pour it on high but stir it not; cover it with a dish, and when it is settled, strew on the top a little fine Sugar mingled with three grains of Ambergreece, and one grain of Musk, and serve it up. (Food Timeline, *My Lord of Carlisle's Sack-posset*)

To make a Compound Posset of Sack, Claret, White-Wine, Ale, Beer, or Juyce of Oranges &c. Take twenty yolks of eggs with a little cream, strain them, and set them by; then have a clean scowred skillet, and put into it a pobble of good sweet cream, and a good quantity of whole cinamon, set it in a boiling on a soft charcoal fire, and stir it continually; the cream having a good taste of the cinnamon, put in the strained eggs and cream into your skillet, stir them together, and give them a warm them have some sack in a deep bason or posset-pot, good store of fine sugar, and some sliced nutmeg; the sack and sugar being warm, take out the cinamon, and pour your eggs and cream very high in to the bason, that it may spatter in it, the strow on loaf sugar. (Food Timeline, *Compound Posset*)

To Make a Posset. Take a Quart of White-wine and a quart of Water, boil whole Spice in them, then take twelve Eggs and put away half the Whites, beat them very well, and take the Wine from the fire, then put in your Eggs and stir them very well, then set it on a slow fire, and stir it till it be thick, sweeten it with Sugar, and strew beaten Spice theron, and serve it in.

To Make a Sack Posset. Take two quarts of Cream and boil it with Whole Spice, then take twelve Eggs well beaten and drained, take the Cream from the fire, and stir in the Eggs, and as much Sugar as will sweeten it, then put in so much Sack as will make it taste well, and set it on the fire again, and let it stand a while, then take a Ladle and raise it up gently from the bottom of the Skillet you make it in, and break it as little as you can, and so do till you see it be thick enough; they put it into a Bason with the Ladle gently; if you do it too much it will whey, and that is not good.

Another way for a Posset. Boil a Quart of Cream as for the other, then take the Yolks of fourteen Eggs and four Whites, beat them and strain them, take the Cream from the fire, and stir in your Eggs, and have your Sack warmed in a Bason, and when the Cream and Eggs are well mixed, put it to the Sack, and sweeten it to your taste with fine Sugar, and let it stand over a Skillet of seething water for a while. (Food Timeline, *To Make a Posset, etc.*)

And here's one more for you, from *The Complete Housewife*, published in 1766 Eliza Smith.

To make Saragosa Wine, or English Sack. To every quart of water put a sprig of rue, and to every gallon a handful of fennel-roots: boil these half an hour, then strain it out, and to every gallon of this liquor put three pounds of honey; boil it two hours, and skim it well; when it is cold, pour it off, and turn it into the vessel, or such casks as is fit for it; keep it a year in the vessel, and then bottle it. It is a very good sack. (Smith, Eliza, p. 214)

Well, what do you think? Sack Possets for your next holiday gathering?? Yeah. Me neither!!

SYLLABUB

Similar to Posset, Syllabub was an English dessert drink that combined dairy products with alcohol. It was originally used as a special beverage for holidays, and it could also be made thick enough to be eaten as a dessert, just like Posset.

Its defining characteristic is the mixing of white wine (or cider or fruit juice) with sweetened cream, so curdling the cream . . . sometimes introduced directly from the cow's udder into a bowl containing the wine and other ingredients. (Food Timeline, *Syllabub: What was Syllabub*)

Season the milk with sugar and white wine, but not enough to curdle it; fill the glasses nearly full, and crown them with whipt cream seasoned. (Randolph, p. 148)

Syllabub.--Traditional recipes call for agitating sweetened cream and milk, well laced with white wine or cherry (or ale or cider), until a great froth is obtained. The agitating is accomplished by methods varying from milking directly from the cow into a bowl of rich cream and wine to the use of a charming 'syllabub churn,' and ingenious device that produces a fine long-lasting froth. In addition to its other virtues, wine serves to lightly curdle the milk and 'set' the fluffy mixture. (Food Timeline, *Syllabub*)

And here's an interesting take on the import of Syllabub in general:

The eighteenth-century fascination with creamy drinks can perhaps only be explained by reference to the ingredients themselves. They are not rare or exotic, but are often either colonial or betray some important British trade connection. In other words, they seem to embody the growing power of the

British Empire, especially now that ordinary housewives can purchase sugar from the West Indies, nutmeg from the Spice Islands, lemons and sherry from Spain. The British housewife is apparently no longer aware that these were once rare and costly ingredients available only to the wealthiest consumers. This syllabub recipe, one of dozens, is something like a cross between an eggnog and a creamy dessert floating on wine. (Food Timeline, *Syllabub from the economic perspective*)

EGG NOG

Egg Nog as we know it today certainly evolved from Posset and Syllabub. Tweaked to adapt to modern tastes and newly available ingredients, it was another creamy dairy based dessert drink laced with alcohol and eggs.

Eggnogg...The drink called eggnog in America may have been an adaptation of milk punch, an old English drink made with milk, eggs, brandy, sugar, and lemon juice. In February 1796, Isaac Weld wrote that he and several other travelers who had stopped in Philadelphia at the same house breakfasted together 'The American travelers, before they pursued their journey, took a hearty draught each, according to custom, of egg-nogg, a mixture composed of new milk, eggs, rum, and sugar, beat up together.'"

- 12 eggs, separated
- 1 cup sugar
- 1 cup bourbon
- 1 cup congnac
- 1/2 teaspoon salt
- 3 pints whipping cream
- nutmeg

- Beat the egg yolks with sugar until thick.
- Slowly add bourbon and cognac.
- Chill several hours.
- Whip egg whites with salt until stiff.
- Whip cream and add broth to egg yolk mixture.
- Chill 1 hour.
- Sprinkle with nutmeg.

Note: For thinner eggnog pour 1 cup of milk in with egg yolks. (Dutton, et al.)

Egg Nogg Break six eggs, separating the whites from the yolks; beat the whites to a stiff froth, put the yolks in a bowl and beat them light. Stir into it slowly, that the spirits may cook the egg, half a pint of rum, or three gills of common brandy; add a quart of rich sweet milk and half a pound of powdered sugar; then stir in the egg froth, and finish by grating nutmeg on the top. (Bryan)

Egg Nogg. (For a party of forty.)

1 dozen eggs.
2 quarts of brandy.
1 pint of Santa Cruz rum.
2 gallons of milk.
1½ lbs. white sugar.

Separate the whites of the eggs from the yolks, beat them separately with an egg-beater until the yolks are well cut up, and the whites assume a light fleecy appearance. Mix all the ingredients (except the whites of the eggs) in a large punch bowl, then let the whites float on top, and ornament with colored sugars. Cool in a tub of ice, and serve. (Thomas)

EGG CAUDLE

Egg Caudle is certainly in the vein of Posset, Syllabub, and Egg Nog, though it is seasoned differently and does not contain dairy. It owes its 'creaminess' to the addition of egg yolks. To be honest, the very name of this beverage makes me kind of squirm. I don't like coddled eggs, so that may be the source of my discomfort. Or, it could be the recipe itself. You decide:

Egg Caudle. Boil ale or beer, scum it, and put to it two or three blades of large mace, some sliced manchet and sugar; then dissolve four or five yolks of eggs with some sack, claret or white-wine, and put into the rest with a little grated nutmeg; fire to a warm and serve it. (May)

Note: what is a 'manchet' you ask? A slice of fine white bread!

MILK PUNCH

Milk Punch could be made with or without the addition of egg. In its simplest form, it was a concoction of sweetened milk and brandy, flavored however you liked.

Here are two recipes, the first without an egg and the second with.

To make fine Milk Punch. Take two quarts of water, one quart of milk, half a pint of lemon-juice, and one quart of brandy, sugar to your taste; put the milk and water together a little warm, then the sugar and the lemon-juice: stir it well together, then the brandy; stir it again, and run it through a flannel bag till it is very fine, then bottle it; it will keep a fortnight or more. (Smith, Eliza, p. 211)

1 fresh egg;
¾ table-spoonful of sugar;
¼ glass of fine shaved ice;
1 wine glass of Brandy;
1 pony glass of St. Croix rum;

fill up the balance with good milk, shake the ingredients together until they become a stiff cream; strain into a large bar glass; grate a little nutmeg on top, and serve. (Johnson)

CORDIALS

Moving away from creamy, eggy drinks (yay!), we move toward a group of sweet dessert beverages, which are all considered cordials. A cordial today can be either non-alcoholic or alcoholic. To settlers, however, it was almost always alcoholic. Cordials were fruit based, very sweet, and often thought to have medicinal qualities.

Cordial. . .it may mean a medicine, or medicinal food or drink, with the property of stimulating the heart and therefore the circulation. The term came also to mean a fruit SYRUP or concentrated and sweetened fruit-based beverage, presumably because it was believed that a preparation of this sort would have this effect. (Davidson, p. 219)

Cordials. . .are made from distilled spirits flavored with fruits, herbs, spices, or other botanicals; sweetened with sugar, honey or other agents; and diluted with wine, water, or other liquids bearing less alcohol than spirits. Cordials are one of the earliest forms of distilled beverages and frequently were used as medicines, since it was believed that the curative properties of certain herbs could be preserved in spirits. . .Early cordials were used both as potable medicines and as liquid ointments for bathing wounds. (Smith, Andrew, p. 167)

SHRUB

While we may think of something green, leafy, and often need-ing a good trim in our gardens, those in the 18th and 19th centuries would have had a completely different image pop into their minds when they heard the word: shrub! It was a very popular cordial made from citrus fruit juice, rum, and sugar. It could be made from other fruit juices, as well, such as cherries and raspberries.

Some variations call for the alcohol to be white wine or brandy, or a mix thereof, and there were even temperance recipes for shrubs that contained vinegar in the place of any kind of alcohol. No matter which alcohol (or vinegar!) was used, however, there was always a great deal of sugar and fruit juice involved.

> . . .in the eighteenth and nineteenth centuries it was a popular drink made from a spirit (usually rum), sugar, and orange or lemon juice. . .The word comes from Arabic shurb beverage, "drink", and is related to English sherbert, sorbet, and syrup. (Food Timeline, *Shrub*)

> Shrub. . .first became popular in the early eighteenth century and was made with brandy, lemon juice and peel, sugar and white wine. Later rum-shrub became very usual; and there were also fancy shrubs flavoured with ground almonds or cur-rant juice. (Food Timeline, *Shrub²*)

> In addition, juices were fermented into flavorful vinegars, and they were used in alcoholic and temperance beverages, includ-ing shrubs, which were composed of fruit juice plus spirits or vinegar. (Smith, Andrew, p. 244)

> Take two quarts brandy and put it in a large bottle, adding to the juice of five lemons, the peels of two, and half a nutmeg; stop it up, let it stand three days, and add to it three pints of

white wine, and a pound and a half of sugar; mix it, strain it twice through a flannel, and bottle it up. It is a pretty wine, and a cordial. (Carter)

RASPBERRY CORDIAL
(which could be considered a variation of Shrub)

To each quart of ripe red raspberries, put one quart of best French brandy, let it remain about a week, then strain it through a sieve or bag, pressing out all the liquid; when you have got as much as you want, reduce the strength to your taste with water, and put a pound of powdered loaf sugar to each gallon; let it stand till refined. Strawberry cordial is made the same way. It destroys the flavour of these fruits to put them on the fire. (Randolph, p. 173)

CARROT ALE

When doing research for this book, I came across this recipe, which I just had to include because it was so unusual. I know that the original settlers were experts in converting just about anything to an alcoholic beverage, but the use of carrots really took me by surprise!

Take of water twelve gallons, carrots twenty-four pounds, treacle four pounds, bran two pounds, dried buck-bean four ounces, and yeast a quarter of a pint. Cut the carrots into thin slices, boil them in the water for an hour, (making up the waste in boiling by the addition of a little water,) strain it, mash up the bran with the carrot water, stir it well to prevent its clotting, add the treacle, let it stand for half an hour, strain and boil the strained liquor for a quarter of an hour with the buck-bean. Finally strain it, and set it aside to cool; when of a sufficient temperature add the yeast, and tun as you would malt beer. This will be found an agreeable and cheap beverage. (Lady, A., p. 659-660)

MULLED CIDER

We wrote in the hot drink section about a non-alcoholic version of mulled cider. Typically, however, the cider would be 'hard' and, therefore, mulled cider was quite a heady blend of alcohol and spices.

According to the *Oxford English Dictionary*, the word 'mulled,' in this context, first applied to mulled wine and it was defined: "Of ale, wine, cider, etc.: Made into a sweetened and spiced hot drink and sometimes thickened with beaten yolk of egg."

I'm not sure why our ancestors had such a fixation with thick, eggy drinks, but it seems evident it was quite a typical addition!

Mulled Cider (Alcoholic)

The website drinkfocus.com gives a great overview:

After the Norman Conquest of 1066, cider consumption became widespread in England and orchards were established specifically to produce cider apples. During medieval times, cider making was an important industry. Monasteries sold vast quantities of their strong, spiced cider to the public. Farm laborers received a cider allowance as part of their wages, and the quantity increased during haymaking. English cider making probably peaked around the mid seventeenth century, when almost every farm had its own cider orchard and press.

. . . .

Early English settlers introduced cider to America by bringing with them seeds for cultivating cider apples. During the colonial period, grains did not thrive well and were costly to import. On the other hand, apple orchards were plentiful, making apples cheap and easily obtainable. As a result, hard cider quickly became one of America's most popular beverages.

Consumption of cider increased steadily during the eighteenth century, due in part to the efforts of the legendary Johnny Appleseed, who planted many apple trees in the Midwest. (Drink Focus)

MULLED WINE

And, lastly, we finish up with mulled wine. Made very similarly to Mulled Cider, here's an excellent explanation of the process:

Hot spiced wine, often called 'mulled wine,' is typically made by simmering red, and occasionally white, wine with a mixture of citrus (juice, slices, or zest from lemons or oranges) and virtually any combination of spices, including cinnamon, clove, allspice, ginger, cardamom, nutmeg, or mace. Wines ranging from dry table wines to sweet ports or fortified wines (strengthened with additional alcohol) are used... Many English, German, Dutch and Scandinavian emigrants who came to America brought these long-held traditions and prepared heated and spiced libations for winter festivals, in particular, Christmas...By the late 1800s these warmed spiced wines had become an integral part of the American Christmas menu, largely because of the strong influence of the middle nineteenth-century novel A Christmas Carol by Charles Dickens. Hot spiced wine was frequently served alongside or in lieu of eggnog enjoyed at middle-class tables, sometimes with appropriate temperance substitutions of fruit juice. (Food Timeline, *Mulled drinks*)

CONCLUSION

So there you have it. . .not an exhaustive list of period beverages, but certainly the lion's share of what would have been within the American pioneer's scope and ability out there on the prairie.

Did you learn something? I sure did as I researched this book! I still can't get over how many pounds of coffee settlers took on their journeys out west and how many weird methods they employed to clarify coffee. The swim bladder of a sturgeon? Really?

And what about the plethora of eggy drinks? Particularly the ones with slightly curdled milk? I'm not sure I'm up to giving some of those recipes a go, thanks just the same.

But it was fun to take a peek. . .not only into the actual period recipes, but the history behind it all, too. From tea parties to remote locations, everything from patriotism to lack of availability impacted what the pioneers drank.

This project confirmed what I already knew, too. The pioneers were resourceful people. Amazingly so. To make coffee out of everything from sweet potato to acorns and fake lemonade when lemons were scarce showed a lot of pluck.

I'm a big fan of pluck. I wonder what other interesting things they got up to?

SOURCES

Arbuckle Coffee Traders, *The Arbuckle Coffee Legend*, http://ar-bucklecoffeetraders.com/legend.html (accessed 2015, now available at http://web.archive.org/web/20130317181424/http:// ar-bucklecoffeetraders.com/legend.html). *See also*, *Our Story*, http://arbucklecoffeetraders.com/about

Atkins, Robert Wayne, *Grandpappy's Basic Acorn Recipes*, http://www.grandpappy.info/racorns.htm (accessed 2013, now available at http://web.archive.org/web/20131106052119/ http://www.grandpappy.info/racorns.htm)

Ayto, John, *The Diner's Dictionary: Word Origins of Food & Drink*, "Buttermilk" [Oxford University Press: Oxford] 2nd Edition 2012 (p. 54), https://books.google.com/books? id=Noi-cAQAAQBAJ

Beeton, Isabella, (1861), *The Book of Household Management*, [S.O. Beeton]

Bradley, Mrs. J.S., *Mrs. Bradley's Housekeeper's Guide*, "Harvest Drink" [H.M. Rulison: Cincinnati] 1853 (p. 99), https://books.google.com/books?id=ye9EAQAAMAAJ

Brown, John Hull (1966), *Early American Beverages*, [Bonanza Books: New York]

Bryan, Mrs. Lettice, *The Kentucky Housewife*, facsimile edition [Applewood Books: Bedford MA] (p. 408), https://books.google.com/books?id=vs5Hjd8mi74C

Cabell Tyree, Marion (Ed.) (1879), *Housekeeping in Old Virginia*, "Chocolate", [John P. Morton & Co.: Louisville, KY] 1879 (1965) reprint (p. 65), https://books.google.com/books? id=ZxUE-AAAAYAAJ

Carter, Susannah (1796), *The Frugal Housewife, or, Complete Woman Cook*, [James Carey: Philadelphia] (p. 126), https://books.google.com/books?id=qrpXAAAAYAAJ

Chase, A.W., M.D. (1860) *Dr. Chase's Recipes, Or Information for Everybody*, 1869 ---*Early American Beverages*, "Root Beer" [A.W. Chase, M.D.: Ann Arbor] 8th Edition (p. 38), https://books.google.com/books?id=WIUFbAcupksC

Child, Mrs. [Lydia] (1832), *The Frugal Housewife*, 9th Edition, [T.T. & J. Tegg: London] (p. 109), https://books.google.com/ books?id=ksNgAAAAcAAJ

Corson, Juliet (1877), *The Cooking Manual of Practical Directions for Economical Every-Day Cookery*, 2010 facsimile edition[Kessinger]

Croly, Mrs. J.C. (1870), *Jennie June's American Cookery Book*, [The American News Company: New York], "Coffee, Tea, etc." & "Wines & Drinks", http://digital.lib.msu.edu/projects/cookbooks/ html/books/book_28.cfm

Davidson, Alan, *Oxford Companion to Food*, [Oxford University Press: Oxford] 3rd edition, 2014, https://books.google.com/ books?id=bIIeBQAAQBAJ

Digby, Kenelm, *The Closet of Sir Kenelm Digby Knight Opened*, (digitized edition) [tredition GmbH], https://books.google.com/ books?id=zzr6mwX5zAUC&pg=PT160

Dixon, Kelly J. (2005), *Boomtown Saloons: Archaeology and History in Virginia City*, [Univ. of Nevada Press: Reno & Las Vegas]

Drink Focus, *History of Apple Cider*, http://drinkfocus.com/history-of-apple-cider/

Dutton, Joan Parry, et al. (1971), *The Williamsburg Cookbook*, [Colonial Williamsburg Foundation:Williamsburg VA] (p. 158-159)

Food Timeline, *Acorns*, qtg *Family Receipt Book* (1819) in *Early American Beverages*, John Hull Brown [Bonanza Books: New York] 1966, http://www.foodtimeline.org/foodbeverages.html #coffeeamerican

Food Timeline, *Beef Tea*, qtg *Cassell's Dictionary of Cookery With Numerous Illustrations* [Cassell, Petter, Galpin & Co.: London] 1875 (p. 65), http://www.foodtimeline.org/foodbeverages.html #beeftea

Food Timeline, *Cider: How old is cider?* qtg *Food and Drink in Britain From the Stone Age to the 19th Century*, C. Anne Wilson [Academy Broadway:Chicago] 1991 (p. 382-383), http://www.foodtimeline.org/foodbeverages.html#cider

Food Timeline, *Cocoa: Modern chocolate begins in 1828*, qtg *Cocoa and Chocolate: A Short History of Their Production and Use* [Walter Baker & Company: Dorchester MA] 1886 (p. 5), http://www.foodtimeline.org/foodbeverages.html#cocoa

Food Timeline, *Coffee Milk*, qtg *Mackenzie's 5,000 Receipts* (p. 100-101), http://www.foodtimeline.org/foodbeverages.html #coffeeamerican

Food Timeline, *Coffee Substitutes*, qtg *Ersatz on the Confederacy: Shortages and Substitutes on the Southern Homefront*, Mary Elizabeth Massey, with a new introduction by Barbara L. Bellows [University of South Carolina Press: Columbia SC] 1952, 1993 (p. 72-72), http://www.foodtimeline.org/foodbeverages.html #coffeeamerican

Food Timeline, *Colonial American Beverages: Hot, non-alcoholic*, qtg *Hung, Strung & Potted: A History of Eating in Colonial America*, Sally Smith Booth [Clarkson Potter: New York] 1971 (p. 199-202), http://www.foodtimeline.org/foodbeverages.html #colonialdrinks

Food Timeline, *Compound Posset*, qtg *The Accomplisht Cook*, Robert May, facsimile 1685 edition [Prospect Books:Devon] 2000 (p. 424-425), http://www.foodtimeline.org/christmasfood.html #posset

Food Timeline, *Dyspepsia Coffee*, qtg *Kansas Home Cook-Book*, Mrs. C.H. Cushing and Mrs. B. Gray, facsimile 1886 edition [Creative Cookbooks: Monterey CA] 2001 (p. 269), http://www.foodtimeline.org/foodbeverages.html#coffeeamerican

Food Timeline, *Early American brewing methods*, qtg *Uncommon Grounds: The History of Coffee and How It Transformed Our World*, Mark Prendergrast [Basic Books: New York] 1999, http://www.foodtimeline.org/foodbeverages.html#coffeeamerican

Food Timeline, *Egg nog: What is Possset?*, qtg *A-Z of Food & Drink*, John Ayto [Oxford University Press: Oxford] 2002 (p. 266), http://www.foodtimeline.org/christmasfood.html#eggnog

Food Timeline, *Hot Chocolate: To Make Chocolate*, qtg *The Experienced English Housekeeper*, Elizabeth Raffald, facsimile 1769 ed. with an intro by Roy Shipperbottom [Southover Press: East Sussex] 1997 (p. 163), http://www.foodtimeline.org/foodbeverages.html#hotchocolate

Food Timeline, *Iced Coffee*, qtg "Paris Gossip," *New York Times*, February 21, 1857 (p. 2), http://www.foodtimeline.org/foodbeverages.html#icedcoffee

Food Timeline, *Mulled drinks*, qtg *Oxford Encyclopedia of Food and Drink in America*, Andrew F. Smith editor [Oxford University Press:New York] 2004, Volume 2 (p. 641-2), http://www.foodtimeline.org/foodbeverages.html#mulled

Food Timeline, *My Lord of Carlisle's Sack-posset*, qtg *The Closet of Sir Kenelme Digbie Opened*, facsimile 1996 London edition [Mallinckrodt Chemical Works reproduction] 1967 (p. 131-132, 134), http://www.foodtimeline.org/christmasfood.html#posset

Food Timeline, *Pioneer Coffee*, qtg *Wagon Wheel Kitchens: Food on the Oregon Trail*, Jacqueline Williams [University of Kansas Press: Lawrence KS] 1993 (p. 41), http://www.foodtimeline.org/foodbeverages.html#coffeeamerican

Food Timeline, *Root Beer*, qtg *Oxford Encyclopedia of Food and Drink in America*, Andrew F. Smith editor [Oxford University Press:New York] 2004, Volume 2 (p. 372-373), http://www.foodtimeline.org/foodbeverages.html#rootbeer

Food Timeline, *Shrub*, qtg *An A-Z of Food & Drink*, John Ayto [Oxford University Press: Oxford] 2002 (p. 312), http://www.foodtimeline.org/foodbeverages.html#shrub

Food Timeline, *Shrub²*, qtg *Food and Drink in Britain From the Stone Age to the 19th Century*, C. Anne Wilson [Academy Broadway: Chicago IL] 1991 (p. 401), http://www.foodtimeline.org/foodbeverages.html#shrub

Food Timeline, *Switchel*, qtg "A Forgotten Drink," *New York Times*, May 24, 1931 (p. SM9), http://www.foodtimeline.org/foodbeverages.html/en-en/pdq.pdf#switchel

Food Timeline, *Syllabub from the economic perspective*, qtg *Food in Early Modern Europe*, Ken Albala [Greenwood Press: Westport CT] 2003 (p. 181), http://www.foodtimeline.org/christmasfood.html#syllabub

Food Timeline, *Syllabub*, qtg *The Virginia Housewife*, Mary Randolph, facsimile 1824 edition with historical notes and commentaries by Karen Hess [University of South Carolina Press:Columbia SC] 1984 (p. 293-294), http://www.foodtimeline.org/christmasfood.html#syllabub

Food Timeline, *Syllabub: What was Syllabub?*, qtg *An A to Z of Food & Drink*, John Ayto [Oxford University Press: Oxford] 2002 (p.332), http://www.foodtimeline.org/christmasfood.html#syllabub

Food Timeline, *To Make a Posset, etc.*, qtg *The Queen-like Closet*, Hannah Wooley, facsimile 1686 reprint [BiblioBazaar] (p. 70-71) http://www.foodtimeline.org/christmasfood.html#posset

Food Timeline, *Virtues of Coffee*, qtg *Family Receipt Book*, 1819 in *Early American Beverages*, John Hull Brown [Bonanza Books: New York] 1966 (p. 100), http://www.foodtimeline.org/foodbeverages.html#coffeeamerican

Food.com, *Barley Tea*, http://www.food.com/recipe/barley-tea-113366

Francatelli, Charles Elmé (1852), *A Plain Cookery Book for the Working Classes*, [London]

George Mason University, *Hard Cider's Mysterious Demise*, http://mason.gmu.edu/~drwillia/cider.html

Gillette, Mrs. F.L. & Ziemann, Hugo (1887), *The White House Cookbook*, http://www.gutenberg.org/files/13923/13923-h/13923-h.htm

Hastings, Lansford W. (1845), *The Emigrants' Guide To Oregon and California*, Applewood Books (reprint).

Hoboes.com, qtg *Drinking in America: A History*, Mark Edward Lender & James Kirby Martin [The Free Press: New York] 1982, http://www.hoboes.com/Politics/Prohibition/Notes/Drinking/

How Products Are Made, *Milk*, http://www.madehow.com/Volume-4/Milk.html

InfoBarrel (Mar 26, 2012), *The Origin of Iced Coffee*, http://www.infobarrel.com/The_Origin_of_Iced_Coffee

Jane Austen's World (Aug 9, 2008), *Hot Chocolate, 18th-19th Century Style*, https://janeaustensworld.wordpress.com/2008/08/09/hot-chocolate-18th-19th-century-style/

Johnson, Harry (1888), *The New and Improved Illustrated Bartenders' Manual; Or: How to Mix Drinks of the Present Style*, [Harry Johnson: New York] (p. 65), https://books.google.com/books?id=pzMEAAAAYAAJ

Lady, A. (1827), *The New London Cookery, And Complete Domestic Guide*, [C Virtue: London] (p. 130-131), https://books.google.com/books?id=bRVdAAAAcAAJ

Lee, Mrs. N.K.M. (1832), *The Cook's Own Book*, [Munroe and Francis: Boston] (p. 19), https://books.google.com/books?id=onEEAAAAYAAJ

Leslie, Miss [Eliza] (1844), *Directions for Cookery in Its Various Branches*, [Carey & Hart: Philadelphia] 20th Edition (p. 391-392), https://books.google.com/books?id=jH0EAAAAYAAJ

Marcy, Randolph B. (1993), *The Prairie Traveler: A Handbook for Overland Expeditions* [Applewood Books, Bedford MA] (Originally published as *A Hand-Book for Overland Expeditions*, [Harper & Brothers: New York] 1859)

May, Robert (1685), *The Accomplisht Cook*, (online transcription), (p. 423/424), http://www.basiccarpentrytechniques.com/Cookery%204/The%20Accomplisht%20Cook/cook2.html#secXXI

Medical Era, The, Vol. VIII., Jan-Dec 1890, [Chicago], "Ginger Drink" (p. 244), https://books.google.com/books?id=LB0CAAAAYAAJ

Murray, George (Sep. 19, 2005), *History of Hot Chocolate*, http://ezinearticles.com/?History-of-Hot-Chocolate&id=72926

Murrey, Thomas J. (1884), *Fifty Soups*, [White, Stokes & Allen]

My Little Prairie Home, *Lemonade Recipe*, http://mylittleprairiehome.com/recipes-beverages-lemonade.asp

My Little Prairie Home, *Pioneer Lemonade Recipe*, http://mylittleprairiehome.com/recipes-beverages-pioneer-lemonade.asp

New York Times (July 16, 1865), *Beef Tea*, qtg *Pall Mall Gazette*, http://www.nytimes.com/1865/07/16/news/beef-tea.html

Owens, Daniel, *Acorns: Are They Safe to Eat?*, http://food-safety.knoji.com/acorns-are-they-safe-to-eat/

Paajanen, Sean, *The History of Hot Chocolate*, http://coffeetea.about.com/cs/chocolate/a/chochistory.htm

Pettigrew, Jane (2001), *A Social History of Tea*, [National Trust: London] (p. 48-51)

Raffald, Elizabeth (1769), *The Experienced English Housekeeper*, facsimile 1769 edition with an introduction by Roy Shipperbottom [Southover Press: East Sussex] 1997 (p. 163)

Randolph, Mrs. Mary (1838), *The Virginia Housewife*, [Plaskitt & Cugle, Baltimore], http://digital.lib.msu.edu/projects/cookbooks/html/books/book_10.cfm

Reddit: AskHistorians, *Southern US Iced Tea Culture*, in comment by cecikierk, https://www.reddit.com/r/AskHistorians/comments/446o3i/southern_us_iced_tea_culture/

Restoration Shed, Sept. 5, 2012, *Brief History of Ginger Beer*, http://www.restorationshed.com/article/brief-history-of-ginger-beer/

Rundell, Maria Eliza Ketelby (1819), *The Family Receipt Book*, "To make Ginger Beer" [Randolph Barnes: Pittsburgh] (p. 85) https://books.google.com/books?id=od8-AAAAYAAJ

Shea, Lisa, *A History of Cider*, WineIntro, http://www.wineintro.com/mulled/cider.html

Simmons, Amelia (1798), *American Cookery*, "For brewing Spruce Beer", [Hartford: Printed for Simeon Butler, Northampton, (1798)] (p. 48) http://digital.lib.msu.edu/projects/cookbooks/coldfusion/display.cfm?ID=amer&PageNum=47

Smith, Andrew F. (Editor), *The Oxford Companion to American Food and Drink*, [Oxford University Press: New York] 2007, (p. 205), https://books.google.com/books?id=GZVweuXhZlkC

Smith, Eliza, (1766), *The Complete Housewife, Or, Accomplished Gentlewoman's Companion*, [Buckland, et al: London], https://books.google.com/books?id=bZ9cAAAAcAAJ

Tea Beyond, *Tea 101 Iced Tea*, qtg *Oxford Encyclopedia of Food and Drink in America*, Andrew F. Smith editor [Oxford University Press: New York] http://teabeyond.blogspot.com/2012/06/tea-101-iced-tea.html

The Kitchn, www.thekitchn.com

The Nibble, *Hot Chocolate History: Page 2a: The History of Chocolate & Hot Cocoa*, http://www.thenibble.com/reviews/main/beverages/cocoas/hot-chocolate-overview2.asp

Thomas, Jerry (1862), *How to Mix Drinks*, [Dick & Fitzgerald: New York] (p. 41), https://books.google.com/books? id=iBo-ZAAAAYAAJ

Vintage Recipes, *Beef Tea*, http://www.vintagerecipes.net/recipes/beverages/beef_tea/

Wikipedia, *Buttermilk*, http://en.wikipedia.org/wiki/Buttermilk

Wikipedia, *Lemon*, http://en.wikipedia.org/wiki/Lemon

Wikipedia, *Whey*, https://en.wikipedia.org/wiki/Whey

Wilcox, Estelle Woods (1877), *Buckeye Cookery and Practical Housekeeping*, [Buckeye Publishing: Minneapolis, Minn], "Drinks", http://digital.lib.msu.edu/projects/cookbooks/html/books/book_33.cfm

Wilder, Laura Ingalls, *Farmer Boy*, "Winter Night"

Wilder, Laura Ingalls, *The Long Winter*, Ch. 1, "Make Hay While the Sun Shines"

wiseGeek, *What is Cambric Tea*, http://www.wisegeek.com/what-is-cambric-tea.htm

ABOUT THE AUTHOR

Robynne Elizabeth Miller is wife to an amazing Brit, mother to a glorious brood of adopted and biological kids, and makes her home in the snowy woods of Northern California's Sierra Nevada Mountains.

Passionate about her family, faith, music and cooking, she can also be found blogging at mylittleprairiehome.com and thepracticalpioneer.com.

She is the author of *From The Mouth of Ma: A Search for Caroline Quiner Ingalls*.

Email

robynne@thepracticalpioneer.com

Web

mylittleprairiehome.com & thepracticalpioneer.com

Twitter

@mlprairiehome

Pinterest

pinterest.com/mlprairiehome/

Have you read:

From the Mouth of Ma:
A Search for Caroline Quiner Ingalls

There's not a whole lot written about Caroline Quiner Ingalls, the mother of famed Little House on the Prairie author, Laura Ingalls Wilder. And I always wondered why. So I set about looking for her. . .in family letters, bits of biography and, mostly, through the words she spoke throughout the Little House series. The Ma I thought I'd find wasn't the one I discovered. Would you like to meet her? I think you'll be happy that you did.

Available at Amazon, Barnes and Noble,
and other fine retailers worldwide.

www.ingramcontent.com/pod-product-compliance
Lightning Source LLC
Chambersburg PA
CBHW051834040426
42447CB00006B/530